TOP *of the* FLOOD

Halfway Through a Fly-Fishing Life

by
TOSH BROWN

DEPARTURE

AUSTIN, TEXAS

ISBN: 978-0-9883852-1-4

Published by:

Departure Publishing LLC
1200 Barton Creek Blvd #6
Austin, TX 78735
(512) 347-8336
www.departurepublishing.com

Edited by Dave Lawton
Design by Departure Publishing LLC
Illustrated by Paul Puckett
Printed by Sheridan Books

"Best Laid Plans," "Van Transfers," "A Matter of Record," "Fishanoma"
and "Creature Comforts" first appeared in *Fly Fishing in Salt Waters*.

"Twelve Hours in the Conch Republic," "The Deke," "Bite or Be
Bitten," "Gentlemen of the Angle," "The Captain's New Clothes,"
"Blow The Man Down," "Hath Hell Frozen?," "Seven Days With Alex,"
and "Cock of the Rock" first appeared in *The Drake*.

"Extremes" first appeared in *Gray's Sporting Journal*.

"Pilot Error" first appeared in *The Fly Fish Journal*.

Top of the Flood

Overheard on Ascension Bay

Angler:

I wonder what the poor people are doing today?

Guide:

They are poling your boat señor.

Preface

Today is my 50th birthday.

While the title of this book might suggest that I'm planning to live to 100, I obviously have no way of knowing that and, truth be told, I'm not really sure I want to live that long. It's more of a suggestion that I'm planning to fish just as many days after 50 as before. My kids are off to college and I'm married to a wonderful woman who loves to travel; so I think that's an attainable goal.

I started fly fishing in the 70's, shooting pictures of fishing in the 80's, and jotting down fish stories in the 90's. At first the writing was nothing more than a way to capture a stream of memories that might complement the 35mm slides that were filling up file folders in my desk. Who knew that words and images would eventually turn into a career?

After college I waved around my UT Business School diploma and got a job in commercial real estate. The tax law changes and financial collapse of 1986 certainly didn't help that career path but, looking back, I now realize that I would have never been successful in that field. Growing up, I loved art and imagery. I made good grades in English. I was awful at math. I hated numbers. I still do. I was born a creative that took a brief detour. I was a right-brain person with a left-brain degree. The impetus to finally change careers was a bit unsettling, but I eventually got it all sorted out.

In this book you'll find a wobbly timeline of fishing stories that begins in the summer of 1976 when I first picked up a fly rod. You may remember a few of these essays from various magazines that I've worked with over the years. The rest were written with this project in mind.

The "halfway" subtitle took some thought, and I'll admit that I ran through a lot of cheesy metaphors while trying to devise a workable theme. For some reason I couldn't get the clichéd sports analogies out of my mind.

He's rounding second and heading for home...

He's at the 30, the 40, the 50...

Lame, I know.

The title eventually came to me on a trip to Belize while we were staked out and eating lunch in the shade of a big mangrove. The tide was dead slack low. The turtle grass tips were showing and as we sat eating our sandwiches, my guide Scully Garbutt said "No hurries. We've got a bit of time before the flood tide starts and everything gets going."

While I started with trout, and I've spent a fair amount of time casting flies in fresh water, I'm most often drawn to the salt. Fly fishing, for me, began like a push of new water onto a low-tide flat. I was hungry and aggressive. Numbers were important. As opportunity arose, I pounced. There were lots of things to catch and I wanted to catch them all.

At a point, the tide rose to a level of contentment. Fishing continued but at a less frenetic pace. I began to slow down and observe and enjoy. Birds became important. I learned to accept bad weather as an inherent risk. I began passing up tailing and rolling fish when the light was good and my camera was within reach. With each passing year the need to catch every fish in front of me slowly diminished.

And now the water has reached its apex. The top of the flood. The moon is big and bright and I'm secure in my place. I'm retracing some paths to chase the fish I really enjoy and I'm making plans to visit new waters and experience some that I haven't yet caught. Very soon the tide will start its ebb and I'll begin riding the water in a different direction. At some point I'll again feel a sense of urgency.

I wish I could predict that you'll find a single point of profound enlightenment in these pages. Some big answer to a big question about life and fly fishing.

Honestly, that's not why I pulled these stories together. Fishing is supposed to be fun, yet many of us have lost sight of that. Some spend their entire lives on the incoming tide; chasing and fussing and flogging the world's waters without ever considering that they may find a bigger reward if they'll just stop casting for a bit and take note of all that's within view. The rods, reels, flies, and fish are a big part of what we do, but over time I've begun to see them more as tactile elements in a much larger scene.

More than anything, I hope you'll be entertained by this book. That's what fly fishing is about: we travel, we cast, we catch fish, we lose fish, we laugh, we meet new people, we witness extraordinary things, and we create memories.

I hope you'll have some fun reading these memories; I've sure enjoyed writing them down.

Tosh Brown
Austin, Texas
July 21st, 2014

Immersion

Pointless. That's how I viewed fly fishing at age twelve. Too many fussy components and a lot of effort required to accomplish a simple task.

I had spent my summers jerking bluegills out from under docks with worms and a hand line and I couldn't grasp why the Montana trout my dad was promoting wouldn't fall for the same technique. My parents were determined to broaden my horizons, but at the time I thought they were plenty broad enough.

The week-long trip in July of 1976 wasn't my first trip to Montana; we'd been vacationing around the state each summer since I was five. Dad would spend most of each day trout fishing while I rode horses and threw rocks in the river.

I'm not sure if the new fly rod, creel, and vest that I got that summer were a part of my dad's overall plan of outdoor indoctrination, or if my mom may have influenced him on the timing of that matter. Regardless of his motive, he had arranged a two-night pack trip into the Beartooth Range, and my older brother and I were booked in with non-refundable vouchers.

I truly loved horses when I was a kid. Over time I would learn why my father hated them. Back home in Texas people rode horses in circles trying to win satin jackets and large belt buckles; in Montana people still rode horses to get places. I thought that was cool.

I don't remember much about the packing and preparation for the trip, probably because I had figured a way to weasel out of it. We lit out on a crisp sunny morning with our guide on the lead horse, and my dad, his friend Chuck Benson, and my brother and me pulling up the rear. The first couple of hours were quite enjoyable. We rode through sweeping valley meadows and stands of alders toward the trailhead that would lead us into the high-country. I was sporting a brand-new pair of Dingo boots and my rod case and bedroll were lashed behind my saddle. I couldn't decide whether I looked more like Curt Gowdy or Hoss Cartwright, so I alternated humming the theme songs from both *Bonanza* and *The American Sportsman*.

My trusty mount was plenty docile on the flatter terrain, but when we reached the box canyon where the Stillwater River roared through a narrow gorge, he got squirrelly and insisted on tightroping the outer three inches of the eight-inch wide trail. The river sounded like a freight train raging through the canyon below, so I tried to manage my fear by fixing my gaze on my dad's horse as it farted its way up the trail in front of me.

I'm pretty sure the ride up the mountain was no more than a few miles, but for a small kid on a big-time expedition, it seemed like we rode most of Lewis and Clark's original route.

Later that afternoon we pitched camp in a stand of spruce next to a lake called Sioux Charley. Our guide told us a story about that name—a Sioux warrior that killed a trapper named Charley, or a Sioux named Charley whose horse fell into the box canyon, something like that.

After the panniers were unpacked and our campsite cleared, we strung up our rods and walked down the hill to the outlet stream below the lake. Dad had an Orvis split cane five-weight and my brother and I were armed with identical Fenwick Ferralite glass rods with Pflueger Medalist reels. In fact, that very outfit still stands in a rod rack next to my desk. The original floating line is stiff and cracked, but otherwise my first official fly rod and reel combo is still in fine shape. I've probably trashed at least a dozen pricey rods and reels since I retired that first one thirty years ago, but the original $20 dollar model is still intact—a little wimpy by today's standards, but still very much operable.

In those days, my father felt that the best way to teach a kid about the outdoors was to provide him with the tools and the opportunity and then get out of the way. "Don't wade too deep, watch those trees on your backcast, and try to keep your fly from waking across the surface." Just enough information to stir my curiosity, but no burdensome details that might confound the big picture.

He pointed out a spot for my brother to fish, and then he stationed me a bit upstream. In hindsight, I suppose he was hoping that my brother would at least make a casual attempt to grab me if I came bobbing past.

My first fly box was made of aluminum with little spring clips inside. I had about eight flies, mostly dries and a couple of nymphs. I was told to dress the Muddler Minnows and Humpys with floatant, and I had two different varieties in my vest: a bottle of liquid that smelled like paint thinner, and a vial of powder that didn't taste at all like sugar.

Wearing blue jeans and Converse low tops, I slipped into the icy water and waded out to a point just shy of ankle-deep. It was a narrow stream, maybe thirty feet wide, and it was full of television-sized boulders and lots of gurgling pockets and holes.

I tucked my rod beneath my arm, opened the paint thinner bottle, and promptly fumbled it into the river. The bottle sank immediately, but the little slick of floatant stayed visible on the surface for quite a stretch downstream.

Reduced, then, to my vial of powder, I shook way too much of it into my palm, spit on my Muddler, and plastered it up like a breaded hushpuppy. At that point I'm not sure that my fly resembled anything a trout would eat, but it clung to the surface like a bloated whale for the remainder of that afternoon.

Having spent a day or two whipping my new rod in the backyard before we left, I was blessed with a rudimentary knowledge and feel for the basic fly-casting motion. For the remainder of that first afternoon, though, my fly spent significantly more time in the air than the water. As long as I was false casting I vaguely resembled someone who knew his way around a trout stream, but when it came time to deliver the fly, my finely choreographed charade would spiral out of control.

On those casts where my fly actually cleared my head and the rod tip, there was no telling how or where it might eventually land. Sometimes it would unroll perfectly, and sometimes it would spiral down in a heap. On some attempts the fly would land delicately before any part of the line or leader touched down (don't ask me how) and on other deliveries I'd crack the whip so violently that my dad and brother would look up to see what I was shooting at.

The low-point of my day came when I had to leave the water and sit down on a rock to unwind a massive macramé project that involved my entire leader, thirty feet of fly line, my hat, and two-thirds of my rod.

During that maddening period of fumbling and cursing, my dad and Chuck were standing upstream catching little rainbows and brookies on every third cast, and my brother was also having a fair amount of success down below. At one point I actually gave up on the massive tangle and started turning over rocks and looking for earthworms.

When I finally cleared the tangle and stepped back into the river, there was a light rain falling and no hint of the brilliant sunshine that had lured us up the mountain that morning. A half-hour later I was still fishless, but casting a bit better, when my father walked downstream and whistled for my brother and me to reel up. The light sprinkle had turned to a steady shower and we were no longer wet just from the knees down.

When we walked back up the hill to camp, we were a bit surprised when we found our outfitter sitting in the rain in his yellow slicker in basically the same position we had left him several hours before.

There was no roaring fire, no shelter, and nothing that resembled dinner. Using spruce bark resin and a handful of dry needles, Chuck was able to get a smoldering fire started, and by the time darkness fell and the rain picked up to a persistent downpour, we had assembled a crude and semi-dry shelter of logs and spruce boughs.

Unfortunately, during our scramble to arrange fire and shelter, we had left our sleeping bags and duffels uncovered. After a quick meal (which I don't really remember, but I'm sure we ate something) we changed from our wet clothes into our damp clothes and then unrolled our soggy sleeping bags for the night.

According to my dad and Chuck, it rained on and off for most of the night. They were sure of that because they never slept for more than three to five minutes at a time. After wiggling and squirming in my bag, I finally found a spot where the raindrops wouldn't drip directly through the lean-to onto my forehead, and from that point I must have bagged at least a few hours of sleep.

It was still raining when we woke the next morning, and the river was roiling out of the lake with the color and consistency of something you might buy at Starbucks.

Getting out of a wet sleeping bag wearing wet clothes was a little easier than getting in, but the discomfort level was still fairly high. There was a brief discussion on the feasibility of staying one more night and hoping that the weather would clear, but at that point no one was willing to gamble.

Other than the persistent rain, I honestly don't remember much about the ride back down the mountain. I do recall that my mom wasn't too happy when we rode in the gate with my dad and Chuck bobbing and slurring inertly in their saddles. Looking back, under similar circumstances, I would've probably swigged an entire flask of bourbon as well.

Two days later, as the news headlines trickled into rural Montana, we learned that our one night of misery paled in comparison to what the residents of Larimer County, Colorado suffered through on that very same night: July 31, 1976.

A freak summer thunderstorm, completely unrelated to our little shower, dumped a foot of rain on the Big Thompson canyon near Estes Park, Colorado. They called it a 300-year flood, an average year's rainfall in just four hours, and it occurred on a weekend when thousands of campers and tourists were in the mountains celebrating Colorado's Centennial and our nation's Bicentennial, as well. Witnesses described a rampaging wall of water carrying massive boulders, automobiles, trees, homes, and human life.

The Big Thompson flood claimed 139 people and tallied over 30 million in property damage. Six more victims were eventually added to the list as "missing and presumed dead." Their bodies were never found. As miserable as we thought we were, our rainy night at Sioux Charley was nothing compared to the horror they suffered through in Colorado.

When school started in September of that year, my teacher asked each of us what we had done on our summer vacation. When I proudly announced that I had gone trout fishing in Montana, the little smartass with the pomade and the mossy overbite sitting next to me snorted and rolled his eyes, "Why'd y'all go all the way down there? Ain't they got those here?"

Thanks, Mom and Dad.

In case I forgot to tell you back then, I had a great time.

The Bass Phase

The Montana trips continued through my middle school years, and while I was never much good at trout fishing, I began to explore my home waters and found a few places to noodle about with a small box of popping bugs that I ordered from the back pages of *Field & Stream*.

Most of my summer bass and panfish days were spent on a small cove behind our family cabin on Cedar Creek Lake. The cove had a hard sand and clay bottom and the shorelines were choked with weedbeds and stumps. Stately oaks and pecans around the fringe provided a little shade, but mostly it was just hot as hell.

My brother and I were proud owners of a 14-foot aluminum Jon boat with a clattering, smoking Johnson outboard. The motor was spray-painted various tones of olive drab because my dad had at one time used the motor on his duck boat. Dubbed "The Green Machine," we spent hours and days in that boat and it offered a stable platform for a dumpy kid that used his whole body to cast a small length of fly line.

On most days, by noon, it was too hot to stand on the Jon boat's decks, so I'd start fairly early when the sun was still low. I'd motor to the far side of the cove and then use a small wooden paddle to ease within range of the weedbeds.

Over time I got fairly good at dropping poppers in the holes and working them along the edges of the weeds. I mostly caught bluegills ("bream" in East Texas parlance) but I'd occasionally catch a small bass that would invariably dive into the thickest part of the weedbed and bury up. My knot tying skills improved significantly when my supply of poppers began to dwindle and replenishment required 4-6 weeks for delivery.

Now, while I've so far painted a somewhat idyllic portrait of my warmwater fishing origins, I can't really claim that I was a fly-fishing purist back in those days. Opportunity was rarely an issue, but a short attention span often stunted the development of my game.

Along with my Fenwick Pflueger fly combo, I'd typically load the Jon boat with a Zebco 303 spincaster, a few lures, and a BB gun. If a water snake poked its head through the weeds I'd drop my backcast and lunge for the BB gun. If the fly rod didn't produce after 3-4 casts I'd pick up the Zebco. If Ronald Tucker was sitting on his dock with his crappie pole, I'd motor over and spray him with a million questions. He knew a lot about arrowheads and trapping coons and trotline fishing. For a kid with lots of time on his hands, that little cove offered a world of wonderment.

On one particular spring weekend trip to Cedar Creek, I found the cove full of tailing and spawning carp. The fly rod was quickly forgotten, as was the BB gun when I figured out that the little copper-plated ammo would only hold its velocity for about three inches under water. Remembering the crossbow I had gotten for Christmas that year, I ran up the hill to the cabin with my mind awhirl with images of massive carp covering the bloody decks of The Green Machine. Mind you, this was long before Rio's Carp Taper fly line, and I'm pretty sure that the Brits and Euros were still hand-rolling their doughballs back then, as well. I was trained to treat carp like the trash that they were.

Over the course of an afternoon, I managed to bury exactly one dozen very expensive crossbow arrows deep into the weedbeds without creasing a single carp.

That night I mailed off my order for a genuine bowfishing rig from *Field & Stream*, complete with a genuine bowfishing reel, barbed arrows, and several miles of string. By the time it arrived, the carp spawn was over.

———

In the summer of 1978, I was stumbling along the awkward cliff edge between kid and teenager. Middle school was done and high school was coming. Girls were important but I had no wheels. Well, actually I did have wheels—but only two, and they required my feet and a greasy chain to get them moving.

My father had made it abundantly clear that the summer of '78 would be my last one of total freedom and screwing around. My brother started working the summer after his freshman year of high school and I was locked in to the same schedule by default. With time on my side, I spent most of that summer at the Corsicana Country Club with my friends. The daily drill was pretty much the same: we laid around the pool, ate burgers, strutted for the girls, did cannon balls off the high dive, and got really sunburned.

One evening in mid-June, some friends and I wandered down to the lake on the golf course after the pool closed. The light was getting low, and I was supposed to be home by "dark-thirty". While we ran around on the greens playing Yank The Bikini String, I noticed a patch of weedy shoreline where bass—BIG BASS—were waking and chasing and blowing up on the surface.

Early the next morning, I roped my fly rod tube to the handlebars of my bike and shoved my reel in one pocket and a box of flies in the other. Pedaling like a demon, I got to the lake just before the fairway sprinklers came on. The bass were in the same place I'd seen them the evening before. My hands shook as I strung up my rod and tied on a big clunky popper with rubber band legs and a balsa head painted like a frog.

On my first cast next to a big boil where something had just been eaten, my fly got sucked under and my loose coils of line began leaving their pile on the ground in crazy whipping loops. When the bass jumped and shook its massive head and my fly popped out, I could only stand there slack-jawed and sweaty while my brain spun through images of tiny dry flies and dink-ass-bug-fed Montana trout that had never ripped fly line through my fingers or made my heart leap into my throat.

For the next two hours I stalked the perimeter of the lake and caught several bass. I lost flies and learned that spare leader material was a necessity. I put impossibly deep bends in my Fenwick 6-weight that made me wonder why one of my father's rods had snapped so easily when I slammed it in the screen door the previous summer. I learned about hook setting and getting a fish on the reel and palming the Pflueger if it was headed for a snag. I figured out that chugging a popper across the surface with fast strips was not the best way to catch bass on a still pond on a hot steamy morning. The slow blooping retrieves with long pauses drove them nuts.

When the sun got high and the bass turned off, I bit off my fly and broke down my rod. When I got back up to the pool where my bike was parked, the lifeguard was plucking June bugs and cigarette butts from the skimmers, and she stopped and stared as I walked by with mud squishing out of my Keds and a long plastic tube tucked under my arm. She was used to seeing me arrive at the pool at noon, not leaving two hours before it opened.

"Where've *you* been?"

"Fishing."

For the remainder of that summer I was torn between my friends at the pool and the bass down the hill. While the girls slathered with coconut oil eventually won out, I did put in

23

enough time with the fish to refine my technique. I also learned that golf course lakes are great for fly fishing because many of the manicured fairways wrapped tightly around the shore, which allowed plenty of room for a backcast. Flags, benches, and ball washers were my only hazards.

Purity of pursuit was again an issue when fishing the golf course, but not because I was easily bored. I'd usually drop the fly rod in the weeds and begin chunking rocks or milling about aimlessly whenever golfers got close. Some of them were near my age and I didn't feel like answering questions about an oddball manner of fishing that didn't involve stinkbait.

One morning my grandfather's golf foursome snuck up on me while I was landing a small bass. They were all fishermen at one point in their lives, so they stopped to watch. When I flipped the bass back into the lake, one of his old cronies said, "You've grown up. I haven't seen you since you were selling those slimy golf balls that you dipped out of the lake over by number five tee-box."

I laughed and walked over to their cart and gave my grandfather a hug.

Those slimy golf balls bought me a lot of popping bugs.

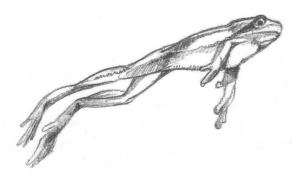

No Country for Frat Boys

The lake, when full, was about 25 acres. It was located on a piece of arid South Texas ranchland, which made it subject to the cruel and irregular cycles of monsoon and drought. Its primary purpose was for watering cattle, but when I first fished there in 1982 it was also full of chunky bass and millions of tiny frogs. After two seasons of rain, the lake had backed up and flooded a series of shallow resacas full of mesquite and prickly pear. The water was dark and clear and the bass were the deepest shades of green, yellow, cream, and black.

Two years later I was sitting in a bar on Austin's 6th Street with Jay and Ethan, a couple of college friends that shared my interest in fishing. It was mid-August and summer classes had just ended. Fraternity rush week was about to start, and since we were two years beyond our own pledgeship, our role in the recruitment of wide-eyed young freshmen was to ply them with unlimited beer and strippers and then keep them out jail. We had three days to kill before all that started and it didn't take long to devise a plan.

The drive to the ranch with the great bass fishing (which I'd promoted to no end) should have taken about four hours. On that particular day we turned it into a sixer, due in part to a busted fan belt on my Ford Bronco and too many stops to supply our epic road trip with all the nonsensical stuff upon which college kids exist.

I started getting nervous when we hit Hondo and the roadside ditches and pastures slowly began fading from the verdant greens of Central Texas, to the crispy browns of a land that hadn't seen measurable rain in seven months. My heart sank when we drove in the ranch gate west of Uvalde and found wilted pastures and skinny cows and two-story dust devils billowing down the chalky two-track roads.

"Looks kinda dry," Ethan noted through a handful of Chili Cheese Fritos that he'd pulled from a five-pound sack.

Jay, ever the optimist, reminded him, "Hey dumbshit, it's August."

The thermometer on the back porch of the old ranch house read 107 when we unlocked the door and unloaded our groceries. It was about 6:30 p.m. and if we were lucky the air conditioner might drop the inside temperature to around 85 before midnight.

Eager to hit the prime fishing time in the evening *cool*, we loaded rods and gear in the truck with about two hours to fish

26

before dark. Figuring that I'd save the big lake with the bigger bass for the next morning's session, I stopped at a smaller stock pond that also held bass when I'd fished it two summers before.

We parked the truck below the dam in a piece of scant shade left by a withered mesquite, but before we could even see the water we were tipped off as to the condition of the bass pond. A blistering wind was blowing in our faces off the top of the dam, and it carried the combined stench of death and cow shit.

"Leave the rods," I told Jay and Ethan, "let's check it out first."

When we topped the dam, three mama cows and a couple of calves broke from their desperate stupor and lumbered away from the mud hole from which they were trying to drink. The once-proud little bass pond with the lush weedbeds and the hovering dragonflies was now a festering slough of filth and decay. Bass and turtle skeletons littered the banks, picked clean by coons and buzzards. You could follow the pond's slow demise since the last rainfall by charting the concentric rings of cattle tracks and dried pies that followed the water's edge as it receded.

We were about to turn and walk away when Jay pointed to the mudhole at the bottom of the pond bed and said, "Check it out."

Roiling about in a befouled slurry of dirt, water, and bovine waste were the two surviving residents of the pond.

"Are those carp?" Ethan asked.

Jay turned and started toward the truck.

The mudhole was about six inches deep and maybe ten feet across. The fish were completely coated in the greenish-brown slime in which they wallowed, and I immediately thought back to an article I'd read that described carp as a *hearty and resilient specie that can survive in water of very poor quality.*

Jay returned with a baitcaster and topwater plug. He walked past us down to the mudhole and lobbed a short cast. Dragging the lure through the mud, he gave it a sharp yank when it reached the first carp and buried the trebles in the fish's back. After dragging it from the mudhole he picked up a piece of mesquite driftwood and cracked it across the fish's head. Three more casts, one more snag and drag, one more dispatched carp.

"Done," he said as he passed us on his way back to the truck.

Short of those two carp sprouting wings, they *were* done, and if I was a carp and given the choice, I'd gladly take a sharp rap to the noggin over death by scavenger.

After a dinner bought from four different convenience stores, we adjourned to the front porch to drink beer and escape the heat. Just before pitch dark, the vapor light out front kicked on and within minutes there was an impressive cloud of moths circling the flickering and humming halo of light at the top of the pole.

As we sat watching the bug show and mulling a plan for the next day, the first Mexican free-tailed bat arrived and began dive-bombing the moth swarm. Within minutes there were two more bats, then three, then five.

Because we were young and of questionable character the discussion immediately turned to the practicability of shooting bats on the wing.

I said, "No way you can hit one of those."

Jay said, "I bet *I* can."

And Ethan said, "Well lets *see* it."

And because we were young and of questionable character, the 20-gauge that we brought along on our bass fishing trip was immediately unsheathed and loaded.

The next morning we got up early, ate more food out of plastic sacks, and loaded a cooler for fishing. I knew the big lake would have more water than the small pond but I had no clue about what shape the bass might be in. There was a brief discussion about a fishing tournament, of sorts, but only because money had changed hands the night before when it was confirmed that bats are indeed impossible to hit with a shotgun.

As we drove across the ranch with dust boiling up behind us and filtering into the truck, Ethan asked, "How far is this place from Mexico?"

"About ten miles to the river if you took off walking," I told him.

He pondered that as he stared out across the scorched pastures. It was 7:30 a.m. and already 80 degrees. "I'll pass..."

I felt a little better about our fishing prospects when we pulled up to the big lake and found it still at about a third of its capacity. The cattle hadn't been moved into that pasture yet, so the water wasn't muddy and there was still a little weed growth around the banks.

What we didn't notice until we'd strung up our rods and approached the shore, was the number of *massive* bullfrogs in the lake. Apparently all the little frogs that I'd seen there two summers ago had grown up and they were now locked in a riparian turf war. The surface of the lake was studded with the snouts and eyeballs of floating bullfrogs. The remaining weed patches were packed with them. With every step along the lake shore, bullfrogs would spook ahead of us. On one stretch of bare, muddy shoreline they were lined up two to three deep and shoulder-to-shoulder facing the water.

Ethan picked up a dirt clod and launched it into the horde, scattering them in all directions. "If this lake gets any lower them frogs'll need bleachers," he noted.

As we fanned out and started prospecting for bass it soon became apparent that the drought had taken its toll. Jay and Ethan were both throwing lures with baitcasters, and I was fishing a Dahlberg Diver on a new 8-weight glass rod that I'd bought the summer before. Over a couple of hours we all caught a few bass, but they were in pretty poor shape. While they attacked practically anything we threw, most of them were pale and nappy with big heads and flat bellies.

By noon, it was pushing 100 degrees and the bass were sulking in the deepest pool next to the dam. We were just about to reel up and head toward the air conditioning when Jay shouted from a ways up the bank from where Ethan and I were fishing. When we turned and looked his way, we saw his rod bent over with the tip bouncing in odd, rhythmic jerks. While we stood watching and speculating on what he might be fighting, he bent down and snatched up a huge bullfrog. By the time we got there, Jay had unhooked the jumper from the little Tiny Torpedo that he was fishing.

"Did you *snag* him?" I asked.

"Hell NO! He was sitting there on the bank and I saw a swirl in front of him that I thought was a bass. When I dropped the lure in there he *dove* on it!"

"What're you gonna do with him?" Ethan asked.

"I'm gonna put him in a croaker sack and them I'm gonna catch me another'n and then we're gonna have us a frog-leg dinner!"

Now, let he who is without sin among us…

We didn't have an actual croaker sack, and I'm not sure I'd know one if I saw one, but our cooler in the back of the truck proved efficient for corralling bullfrogs.

For the remainder of that day, and most of the next, we three sports developed and perfected myriad techniques for stalking, casting to, and catching bullfrogs on rod and reel. Since this is a fly-fishing book I won't expound on Jay and Ethan's techniques for duping amphibians with conventional gear; but here's what you need to know about the bullfrog on a fly game.

While wary and elusive, the American bullfrog (*Rana catesbeiana*) is quite aggressive, especially when they outnumber their food source. While they mainly eat bugs and small aquatic life, an adult bullfrog will readily pursue larger prey.

I know that may sound like an article out of *Fly Fisherman*, but I actually made it up.

What I did confirm after two days of stalking bullfrogs is that stealth and presentation are much more important than fly choice. It didn't really matter what I was casting as long as I laid it down softly within one or two hops of the frog. Poppers, streamers, Woolly Buggers; it didn't matter. For some reason, though, the floaters in the pond weren't nearly as aggressive as the bank sitters. Once I got that major point dialed in, the details were a matter of trial and error.

Since none of my bass flies had decent weedguards, I spent most of the time stalking sitters that were on bare dirt or in real shallow water over clean mud. With any vegetation about, the fly would invariably snag during the all-important retrieve. Here's how it typically went:

I'd pick out a bank sitter and begin my stalk. They mostly sat facing the lake within a few inches of the water. I quickly learned that their peripheral vision on land wasn't that keen. If I snuck straight down the bank right at the water's edge I couldn't get within fifty feet without spooking the frog. If I backed away from the shore a few feet and came at them from their rear quarter I could usually get much closer. This also presented a good angle for landing the fly. If I dropped it on the bank between me and the frog, he'd sometimes turn and attack, but not always. If I over-shot my cast and leadered the frog, he'd spook every time. The sweet spot, I soon learned, was the skinny water right in front of his nose. Too far out and he wouldn't go after it; 10-12 inches seemed to be the perfect distance.

So, if I made a successful stalk, and I put the fly in place without spooking the frog, I'd then have to figure out what mood he was in. A fast, noisy retrieve was no good; they'd turn a back-flip trying to get away from that. What did seem to work was a typical calm-water bass retrieve; land the fly soft, let the rings completely disperse, and then give it a little jiggle.

The first time I tried that technique with the Dahlberg is indelibly fixed in my mind. It was a big bull-honker and he was sitting next to a small log, which further narrowed my target zone. My cast was a little long, and the fly actually landed atop the log, but with a gentle nudge I was able to slip it into the water without it snagging. When the fly slid in the water, the frog turned and squared up on it, still about a foot away. I paused…a long five count…and then slowly twitched the fly away from the log. With one hop, he was on it, and it startled me so badly that I'm surprised I didn't trout-set him.

What happened next was totally unexpected. I was gathering up my line to strip-set, but realized that he didn't have the fly in his mouth; he had actually used his little t-rex forearms to pin it down in the mud. Worried that I'd foul-hook him, I held my breath and waited for his next move. After what seemed like an eternity, the frog actually jerked the fly out of the mud and used both hands to stuff it in his mouth like a fat lady eating Milk Duds. When I reared back and gave him the steel, he reacted exactly as I hoped he would. With one incredibly long jump, he was in the water and kicking away at top speed. It wasn't a steady bass run with crazy jumps; it was more of a jolting, bucking experience that made my little click and pawl reel buzz in rhythm with his scissor kicks. It wasn't an extremely long and powerful fight, but it was damn exciting.

When the three of us finally called it a wrap, we had filled up half of our cooler with frogs. I don't recall how many we caught, but it was heavy when we loaded it into the truck. Fortunately, Jay knew all about cleaning bullfrogs so it wasn't too much of a chore to get them dressed, skinned, and iced down.

A few weeks later, back in Austin, we fired up Jay's fish cooker and invited friends over. With hot oil and sticky batter and frog legs and cold beer and the Longhorns on TV, we ate like sovereigns without realizing how good we had it.

Not long after that we all had diplomas and jobs, and fishing for bullfrogs seemed distant and silly.

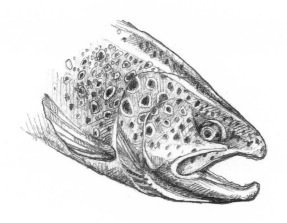

Reboot

During my junior year in college, my father came up with the idea of an annual guy's fishing trip for him and me, my brother, and brother-in-law. Having never traveled further than Montana's Stillwater Valley, the first trip was to Alberta's Bow River in the summer of 1985.

The trip involved hotel rooms in Calgary and daily floats with a guide. The trout were much bigger than those we had found in Montana, and our guide explained that their piggish build was a result of the Bow's prolific aquatic growth provided by Calgary's water treatment facility. Or as one fly shop owner in Calgary described the Bow, "Where the affluent fish the effluent."

The Bow was big and wide where it cut a meandering swath through Alberta's wheat country, and we really enjoyed the experience of trout that could pull string off a reel. While the guides were excellent boatmen and great to spend a day with, I don't remember them being particularly long on technical fishing advice. On one morning we approached a run where the guide wanted us to switch over to Woolly Buggers and dredge for some big browns that he'd found there. When my dad asked him how he should fish the streamer, the guide answered, "Spank the fuckin' bank."

On our return flight home there were thunderstorms stretched across North Texas and our descent into DFW was a little bumpy. On final we were lined up with the runway with a huge thunderstorm just west of the airport. What happened next is a bit hard to explain, but it started with a pressure buildup in my ears. I couldn't pop it by opening my mouth like I typically could when flying, so the pressure continued to build to a point where I was getting really uncomfortable. With the landing gear down and the plane settling in for touchdown, I reached up and did the old nose clamp blow, and that's when all hell broke loose.

When my left ear finally popped, my entire field of vision suddenly rotated 180 degrees to the right on the vertical axis. Having never experienced that sensation, I thought that a blast of wind had hit the plane. My brain told me that since my field of vision had flipped, that I was also inverted, and if I was strapped into an airplane seat, then that meant the goshdarn airplane was inverted too. So, like anyone who thought they were about to die in a plane crash, I began gasping and flailing and bracing for impact.

Imagine my surprise when those actions caused my right ear to pop, and my inverted view of the airplane cabin immediately rotated back to normal. Seconds later the wheels gently scuffed the runway and we landed smooth and easy.

When I finally gathered my wits enough to look around and assess the situation, I found everyone within two rows looking at me like I'd completely flipped out. Which I had.

"Sorry, I thought we were crashing."

Two weeks later I was driving to class in Austin when I had a dizzy spell that forced me to pull over in traffic.

A month after that I was visiting my parents and fell on my ass when I tried to stand up from a chair.

Not long after, I was standing at my fridge drinking orange juice out of the jug and when I leaned my head back to get that last swig, I fell backward. Oddly, though, I never had the sensation that I was falling, which meant that I made no effort to catch myself before the back of my head hit the kitchen floor. It was cheap vinyl, so there was no blood, but that night I called my folks and told them I was going to the doctor.

He looked in my ears, cleaned out some wax, looked in my nose, commented on its construction, and then said, "You've got a middle ear infection, take some pills."

A week later the dizzy spells returned with frequency.

Over the next few months I traveled the state between specialists in Austin, Dallas and Houston. One of them, a neuro-surgeon at Methodist Hospital, suggested a CAT Scan. That showed him something, but not enough, so he suggested a new technology called MRI.

I should note that early MRI machines weren't quite as roomy as those in operation today. When the nurse offered me a sedative I declined, but later wished I'd taken it. The tube was so narrow that I had to scrunch my shoulders going in, and once in place my nose was only about two inches from the top surface. I passed the time by thinking of sausage making.

A few days later I got a call from the doctor and he had found exactly what he was expecting. In the auditory canal that runs from my right ear to my brain, was a tumor about the size of a quarter. It was called an Acoustic Neuroma. He suspected that it was benign, but it was wrapped around the nerve chain that controls hearing, balance, and facial movements. While my hearing was fine and I didn't have a droopy face, that little fleshy annoyance was the cause of my falling down at inopportune times.

"It needs to come out," he said. So in mid-February I was wheeled into surgery.

Now, in case you've forgotten, or if you've yet to reach this point in time, age twenty-two for most American males falls toward the end of the Bulletproof Phase. You're probably done with college, there may be a job on the horizon, and the burden of adulthood is hovering above your shoulders but not yet weighing you down. That's exactly where I was. And that's why the notion of having a hole sawed in my skull didn't seem like much of a deal.

Ain't no step for a stepper, right?

After several hours on the table, the doc walked into the waiting room and told my folks, "We got most of it, but not all of it. He should be okay."

For the first 24 hours I was under heavy sedation in ICU.

My folks were allowed in every four hours for a quick visit, but I don't remember any of that. My first recollection, post-surgery, was the night nurse whose ass was wider than my bed. That wouldn't have posed a problem if I didn't have spinal fluid leaking from my right ear, which caused a pressure imbalance and unimaginable headaches. The ICU room was tiny, and she wasn't, and every time she moved in the room she'd bump my bed. Every bump of the bed sent lightning bolts into my brain.

When my mom and dad came in the next morning they asked if they could bring me anything. I asked for a skinny nurse.

After another week in the hospital and some physical therapy to reprogram my walking and balance mechanisms, I was sent home to continue my bulletproof life. I went back to work in the commercial real estate office that had recently hired me, and resumed my life of young bachelorhood in a great city with lots of fun stuff to do. I had an impressive scar and a funky haircut, and I ended up with total hearing loss in my right ear, but beyond that I was good to go.

Over the next couple of years, we made two more trips to the Bow River and I found a few golf course ponds around Austin with really nice bass. Those country clubs were a bit more prickly about access, but I managed.

In 1988 I met a pretty girl named Kathy. Not long after that I went back to Houston for a follow up MRI and got some startling news. The tumor had grown back and it was bigger than before.

A month later I was back in surgery, a week after that I was back home. The doctor promised that they'd gotten it all, and

I was still employed, but things were different. I was angry and I was unsettled. I no longer felt bulletproof and I hated my job. The economy was awful and properties weren't selling. I found myself moping around and wondering if life was indeed as short as so many claimed.

Having just recently proposed to Kathy, I can imagine her surprise when I told her that I was thinking about a career change. Being the forever calm and wonderful and supportive person that attracted me to her in the first place, she said, "If that's how you feel then go for it." And then she asked, "What is it that you *really* enjoy doing?"

I'd already ruled out a roadside jerky stand, so I said, "I *really* like to hunt and fish."

She could have jumped up and run screaming through the hedge at that point, but she didn't, and I probably don't tell her often enough how much I appreciate that.

Since I was an avid consumer of outdoor magazines at the time, my mailing address was farmed out to other sporting-related industries. One day a thick and glossy catalog arrived from a travel agency specializing in fly fishing and wingshooting. I poured through it several times and immersed myself in the stunning photography and the flowery promotional text for each destination. I figured out that they worked on commission and then I looked at the prices of the trips and ran the numbers in my head. I then compared those numbers to what I was not earning in commission trying to sell real estate at a time when no one wanted to buy it.

I could do this. I know people who go to lodges like these. People like to have fun and I could sell fun. I could start small with a few destinations, work out of my house, build it up from scratch. I'll then visit more lodges and outfitters as client demand dictates. I love to bird hunt, and I've caught trout, and bass...and bullfrogs...

A while later I walked into my employer's office and said, "I really appreciate the opportunity, but I'm moving on."

The Iliamna Egg Wars

In the late 80's there was a clandestine battle brewing on a handful of rivers in the Bristol Bay region of Alaska.

The Iliamna and Katmai drainages attract huge numbers of spawning sockeye salmon, and the native rainbow trout thrive on the by-products of the annual migration: millions of salmon eggs are deposited in the rivers each summer, and millions of hatchling salmon fry emerge each spring.

By late August of each year, the sockeye spawn begins to wane and the rainbows switch into desperation mode. The days get shorter and the trout know that it's time to fatten up for the winter. They set up downstream from the active salmon redds and slurp up every egg that washes past. With their bellies distended, and eggs literally spilling from their mouths, these trout will still move a considerable distance across current to snag another little pink orb of salmon protein.

It wasn't, however, the abundance of slob trout in those waters that caused the ruckus back in the eighties; they'd been feeding on the salmon spawn and growing huge forever. Instead, what raised the ire of a sector of anglers and actually sparked the battle was a controversial new technique used to catch those trout.

After hanging out my travel agency shingle in the spring of 1989, one of my first priorities was to visit and learn about the Bristol Bay fisheries. Even though mine was a new agency, I found most of the lodge owners eager to work with someone who might bring them new business. With an itinerary of three lodges to visit over a 12-day period, I booked a flight to Anchorage, and then a puddle-jumper to King Salmon.

For many years, the fly of choice for catching the big fall rainbows was a simple puff of pinkish orange yarn, spun on a hook, and trimmed into the shape of a salmon egg. I'm not sure who tied the first Iliamna Pinky, but it was easy to fish and incredibly effective on egg-drunk rainbows.

On that first trip to Alaska in the fall of '89, all three lodges that I visited listed the Pinky as a must-have fly for catching those big September trout. I showed up with two-dozen Pinkies in varying sizes and colors, but I learned on arrival that one of the lodges had recently perfected a new egg-fly technique for catching those giant fall rainbows. Like many other anglers who fished under their tutelage and witnessed the revolution first-hand, I was sworn to secrecy on the technique, the name, and the location of those rivers. The big rainbows in those waters were already well-known and the crowds were steadily building on those runs.

Now, two-dozen years later, the cat is unfortunately miles out of the bag as the technique was eventually scribed, photographed, and filmed from every imaginable angle. So for that reason I'll go ahead and relate my experience, but I won't divulge the rivers, the lodge, and the guides by proper name. It's just better that way.

On our first day, we were flown out to Brooks Camp for what I later learned was an orientation, of sorts. First we got a lecture on bear/fisherman etiquette from the presiding park ranger. Then we were shown the infamous Brooks Falls, which is like McDonald's for bears and *The Little Shop of Horrors* for salmon. After moving downriver to a spot void of snorkeling carnivores, the guides pointed out the sockeyes, which weren't too hard to spot in their crimson spawning wear. Below them they showed us the rainbows that were juking and jockeying for position downcurrent from the spawning beds.

Because there were anglers around from other lodges, our guides chose to keep their secret weapon under wraps for that first day. We tied Pinkies on 6-weights, dead drifted them under bobbers, and caught lots of beautiful rainbows. Most of them were much bigger than any trout I'd ever seen in Montana or Alberta.

At dinner, that night, the schedule was posted for the next day, and the guide to which I was assigned mentioned over dessert that the next day's fishing would be substantially different.

At dawn we were flown to a meandering tundra river and dropped off for a day of walk-and-wade fishing. The banks were fouled with bear scat and spawned-out sockeye carcasses. We were the only anglers within view but the guide still wasn't taking any chances.

Looking around before unzipping his jacket, he pulled out a plastic canister and clutched it close to his chest. Inside were hundreds of small plastic beads that were painted/dyed in every imaginable salmon egg shade from creamy orange to blood red. After walking down the bank and examining a few errant sockeye eggs that had washed from their beds, the guide selected a bead color that exactly matched the eggs he had found. From there he slid the bead on my leader, clamped a split-shot about a foot above it, and tied a small bare hook beneath that.

"These fish are bigger and smarter than what you saw yesterday at Brooks," he said. "No bobbers today so you need to pay attention. These beads behave in water almost exactly like a real egg, same buoyancy...but still...these fish are different."

He handed back my rod and motioned for me to follow him. At the beginning of the first run we found a small knot of spawning sockeyes. Below them was a deep chute alongside a high cut bank. It was cloudy and I couldn't immediately spot any trout, but that didn't matter.

"Here's the drill," said the guide. "We're blind fishing now, so it's a matter of putting that egg in just the right current seam, giving it a mend, and then watching for the grab."

I stripped out some line and we waded out a few feet.

"Can you see the current seam there where it follows the deeper water?"

"Yep."

"Make a cast about 45 degrees upstream, give it a quick mend, and let your egg drift right down that line."

My first cast was long and the fly tumbled into the fast water and ripped through the seam. The second cast was on target but my mend was weak. He called the third cast good and then told me to watch the end of my fly line for any slight—

"THERE!"

When I set the hook my lined hissed upstream for about five yards before a rainbow trout with the girth of a raccoon came cartwheeling out of the run.

"Get him on the reel quick, and be ready to chase him!" the guide yelled.

At just the point where my final loop of slack line jumped tight on the reel, the trout turned and ran through the tailout and into the next run. This was a new experience for me. Jogging and reeling down the gravel bar I could see my backing beneath just a few wraps of fly line.

When we caught up to the fish it was sulking in a deep slot next to the far bank. With some side pressure I was able to turn its head back into the main current, and after a couple more short dashes the trout finally rolled over on a shallow gravel bar. I was speechless. I thought the trout at Brooks were huge. The guide stretched a tape on him at 26 inches and after a quick photo we released him back into the run.

Over the next three hours I caught more big rainbows than I had ever imagined possible. After the first hour an 18-incher became an annoying skater. I soon learned that the measuring stick on that particular river was a 30-inch trout; that's the fish by which you judge all others.

Just before noon we rounded a bend and found another party of two anglers and their guide fishing the run below us. "We'll stop here and have lunch," the guide said. "I want to let them clear out and give that spot some time to rest."

He dropped his pack on the gravel bar and we dug out sandwiches and pasta salad and cookies. It was cold and blowing with spitting rain and the thermos of hot soup was a godsend. When we finished our lunch the guide walked down to visit with the other party as they were packing up to leave. When he walked back up to where I was stretched out on the gravel bar, he had a sheepish grin on his face. "That run's loaded with trout," he said.

"Yeah?"

"They've been fishing Pinkies and leeches and they've only moved a couple of fish."

When the other group was well down river, we loaded up the pack and walked down to the head of the run. It was another deep chute with a mob of spawning sockeyes at the head. After a quick glance around, another bead was selected that was a shade darker than the one we had fished all morning. "These are fresh beds with darker eggs," he said. "We need to match the hatch… so to speak."

I asked him, "So it doesn't bother you that they've already fished this?"

"Normally, yes, but not anymore. These beads are a game changer."

And he was right. It was a short piece of water but we basically stood in one place and fished it until the plane arrived at 4:00. Trout, after trout, after trout.

"Don't get me wrong," the guide said as we were hiking up the hill to the plane. "Those Pinkies are still a great fly in most places, but that waterlogged fuzz lashed on a hook just doesn't act quite right in the current. There aren't many rivers up here with trout this size. It's a short growing season so these big rainbows are old dudes. By the time they get two-feet long, they've seen a lot of real eggs and a lot of fakes."

Back at the lodge that night, he gave me an abbreviated history on the development of the beads. "I suspect a couple of other lodges might know about them, but everyone is keeping it under really tight wraps," he explained. "We've been telling all of our guests to keep it mum and not show photos of the beads. We work really hard up here to put our guests on fish and we hope they appreciate our efforts."

When I left that lodge and arrived at my next stop, I was immediately quizzed by a couple of the guides working there. They wanted to know which rivers I'd fished and with which guides. Oddly, they never asked about the flies that we used.

For the remainder of that trip I got to fish several more great rivers and met some wonderful guides and lodge owners. I ended up sending clients to each of them over the years, and I eagerly listened to the fishing reports when a client returned from a fall rainbow trip. There was never a mention of beads until one of the fly-fishing magazines ran a story in, or around, 1993. At that point the gloves came off.

Alaskan lodges and guides were screaming at each other, with some of the old traditionalists crying foul and claiming that fly fishing is about hair and feathers, and not orbs of plastic. Crowds on the "big trout rivers" became an issue, with float-planes dog-fighting for landing spots and anglers boot-racing each other to the prime runs. There were protests to the State of Alaska to make bead-fishing illegal. Some claimed that the use of beads resulted in too many gut-hooked trout, while the bead fishers decried the punctured eyes and shredded mandibles on fish caught multiple times with big barbed streamer hooks. It got ugly, and it stayed ugly for a few years.

In 1997, I made a return trip to Iliamna and hosted a group of clients for a week of fall rainbows. The Egg Wars had wound down by then and everyone was using beads and every-one was catching fish.

In the Anchorage airport on the way back to Austin, I was waiting to check in for my flight when an elderly gentleman saw my rod tube and asked where I'd been fishing. It turns out we were on the same river, but he was fishing from a different lodge. When I asked about his week, he smiled and said, "I caught the trout of a lifetime, a big hen rainbow that was 32 inches long with a 17-inch girth." I congratulated him on his catch and we swapped business cards.

A week later I got two photos in the mail from him. One was a shot of he and his guide grinning proudly with the trout, and the second shot was a close-up of just the fish. In the corner of its mouth I could plainly see the fly. It was a small waterlogged clump of fuzz called an Iliamna Pinky.

Best Laid Plans

Back in the early 90's the bonefish travel boom was climbing toward a precipitous peak. Books, videos, magazine articles, and Saturday morning TV were the combined impetus, and outfitters were scrambling abroad like maniacal dock rats trying to cash in.

While anglers continually buzzed my office asking about flats-casting opportunities, my mailbox filled up with brochures from promoters claiming that their new lodge was the hub of the bonefishing universe.

Driven by the combination of client demand and perceived opportunity, I departed in June of 1991 on another whirlwind lodge tour. I'd visit several outfitters in one trip, check out their programs, and dash back home to report my findings.

My first stop on Grand Bahama found an established lodge with a veteran guide team, good boats, and great fishing.

From there I fished for three days with Rupert Leadon on Andros (yes, he played the saw while I was there) and then I was scheduled for a final stop in the Exumas.

Unfortunately, Bahamasair had decided to cancel a few key flights without telling me, so short of swimming, rowing, or diverting by air through the Pacific Northwest, there was no chance of keeping my original schedule. A voucher was issued by the airline, but now I had a decision to make: cash in and detour to another island, or marinate in a Nassau casino for two days.

"What else you got?" I asked the surly, yet indifferent agent at the Bahamasair counter.

Walker's Cay was better known for their offshore fishing, but they had recently begun promoting their bonefish opportunities. It's a small island at the northern end of the chain with a few nice flats and quick access to the bluewater trenches. Their airport runway is shorter than a carrier deck, and oddly they've made no effort to haul away the crumpled fuselages rusting in the mangroves just shy of the mark.

When I met the fishing manager the next morning at the dock, he was sorry to inform me that their "top guide" had the sniffles, but that his father would be happy to take me fishing. He pointed to an elderly gentleman over by the swimming pool that was raking up sea grape leaves with no particular pattern or urgency.

I didn't want to be rude, but I wondered if the groundskeeper knew much about bonefish outside of great bottom-muddling hordes. The manager must have sensed my apprehension as I stood pondering and chewing my lip, and thankfully he offered another option before I had to ask, "What else you got?" for the second time in 24 hours.

"My nephew, Harvey, has been fly fishing a bit," he offered hesitantly. "He handles a boat well, but I'm not sure he's ready for guiding."

Twenty minutes later, Harvey and I were speeding away from the dock in a gleaming new Dolphin skiff and bee-lining for a cluster of keys on the horizon. He was nattily dressed in a papaya colored Tarponwear shirt, and he acted every bit the part of an accomplished fly-fishing guide.

When the first flat came into view, he deftly threaded the skiff through a maze of coral heads, crossed the edge of the bar, and then ran us aground at twenty knots.

"Oh glory Jesus!" he exclaimed as the motor ground to a halt. "Dat tide has really run out today!"

I picked myself up from the floor-well and peeked over the gunnel toward the mangroves. The water was lapping under the foliage where nary a crusty red root was showing.

Harvey was obviously embarrassed, but still exuding confidence. "Well, we can either push off this bar and try another flat, or we can wade around here and see if dey's any bones at home."

I didn't want to tell him how to run his day, but I couldn't imagine a bonefish hanging around after an outboard had plowed a forty-foot trench of marl through its living room.

"How about over there?" I pointed across the channel.

He studied the distant flat for a moment, and then hopped out of the boat to push us off the bar. "Dat looks better anyhah," he agreed. "The tide's too low on dis flat."

On that day I was far from accomplished, with only five days of bonefishing to my credit, but I had seen enough of them to know what they looked like swimming over white sand in good light. Harvey had just re-mounted his poling platform when I saw a pair wheel and spook that had been cruising right toward us.

"Two boxfish goin' away fast!" Harvey pointed out. "That's a good sign 'cause bones and boxes like de same type of flat."

I politely held my tongue, but realized at that moment that I'd have to begin creating my own opportunities. After fifty yards of loud and crunchy poling, a big single rounded a point of mangroves and began quartering our direction.

"There's one…" I whispered, starting my cast.

"Nah, das a cuda," Harvey hissed.

I managed a decent downwind lob and dropped the fly about three feet in front of the bonefish. It veered and accelerated toward the fly, but just before it tipped up to eat, Harvey's push pole came sailing over my left shoulder and javelined into the mud with a violent KER-BLOOSH! The terrified bonefish departed the flat like its ass was on fire.

"That'll teach dat nasty cuda about eatin' flies!" Harvey whooped. "He'd cut it off clean like a knife, Mista Brown! Next time let's hold off 'til we know it's a bonefish!"

For the next seven hours the exercise was pretty much the same. I tried to hone my fish spotting skills, and Harvey managed to spook every fish I pointed out. We would race up to a flat and he would grab his pole and start pounding us along with bonefish scattering like cockroaches just out of casting range. I did manage to catch one decent fish during our lunch break. It was an underachiever that snuck up on us while Harvey was eating his conch salad.

That night at dinner, I was seated at a table near the bar and wondering what surprise Bahamasair might have in store for me the next day.

When my waiter approached from behind and delivered a menu over my shoulder, I recognized his voice before we ever made eye contact.

"Good evenin' sah. My name is Harvey and I'll be your— HEY it's Mista Brown! I bet you didn't spot me in my evenin' get-up."

He was pumping my hand madly and beaming like we hadn't seen each other in years. I complimented him on his uniform, and he quickly explained that table waiting was only a part-time gig, and that he'd be ditching the linen jacket when his calendar filled up with anglers.

Several years later, at a different dinner table in a different country, I overheard a couple of guests comparing notes on the Bahamas and the little island with the short runway.

"Oh yeaaah, I went there back in '96 and fished a couple of days with a guide named Bonefish Harvey."

"You do any good?"

"Not really. He was better at folding napkins than spotting fish."

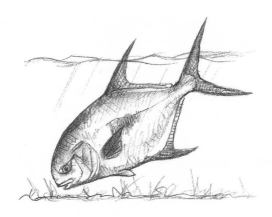

Van Transfers

Bob from Boston briefly glanced our way as we pulled in beneath the ornate stone portico of the Ritz Carlton Cancun. He was obviously waiting for someone to pick him up, but judging by his facial expression he was hoping that it wasn't us.

He quickly returned his gaze toward the cobbled entry drive to the hotel, but then he glanced back again and noticed that the person in the passenger's seat (me) was dressed to go fishing. You could almost see the eager anticipation of a great fishing day draining right out of his body. He obviously wasn't expecting such a primitive mode of transportation.

Humberto (Beto) Marfil, our head guide and driver, waved at the well-heeled sport standing next to his pile of fishing gear. Bob pretended not to see Beto's wave, but he couldn't ignore the rest of us staring impatiently at him through the van windows. It appeared that the angler from Boston's worst nightmare had just come true.

He startled noticeably when the old engine backfired like a musket shot and coughed up a cloud of noxious yellow smoke, but he continued his cautious approach toward the van.

"Ahhhhhh...*Bee-toe*...is it? Are you Señor *Bee-toe* Marfil?" he asked, as he double-checked the name on the itinerary that his travel agent had prepared. "I'm supposed to meet a fellow here named *Bee-toe* at 6:30; you wouldn't be him would you?"

Beto looked at me, perplexed, probably because he had never been referred to as a person who "wouldn't be him."

"That's him," I spoke up realizing that Beto was obviously still uncertain as to who was exactly whom at that moment. "That's *Beto*—with an "eh"—and I'm Tosh. Not sure what his real name is, but the guide in the back goes by "Sand Flea."

"Okay...okay...then...super!" he said smiling fretfully. "Bee-toe, Tosh, and Sand Flea. I'm Bob from Boston and it looks like you guys must be my ride."

Our destination that morning was a system of flats and mangrove lagoons north of Cancun that stretched for about thirty miles up to Cabo Catoche at the northernmost tip of the Yucatan Peninsula.

"So how's the fishing been, fellas?" Bob asked excitedly as Beto pulled out of the Ritz and merged into the early morning traffic on the main boulevard. "My travel agent told me that I had a good chance of catching a grand slam on the fly at this place."

I wasn't about to get involved in that exchange, so I

deferred to Beto who was driving along and pretending that he didn't hear the question.

"Bueno," Beto finally replied after I nudged him back into the conversation with my elbow. "Many gran-slams. Muchas, shark, sting-aray and needlefeesh for you, Bob."

I tried to hold it back, but when Sand Flea erupted in laughter in the back seat, I launched a spray of coffee through my nose. Bob forced a laugh as well, but he was obviously not as amused as the rest of us. For the remainder of the ride he directed all his questions directly at me.

The van we were crammed into was of VW manufacture, unknown vintage, and its cast was several different shades of blue. It didn't come from the factory that way, nor was it a reflection of Beto's artistic expression. Whenever it needed painting there was simply never enough of one color lying around to finish the job.

The A/C didn't work and the horn consisted of two bare wires hanging under the dash that had to be touched together to obtain the desired result. Fortunately, our daily trips to and from the lagoon didn't involve too many busy intersections or traffic circles. In most Mexican cities, the person who taps his horn first at an intersection is the one who gets to go first; never mind the lights, the signage, or which car actually arrived there first. Had this commute involved a trip through the gridlock of downtown Cancun, we would have been at a serious disadvantage with that manual horn arrangement.

If a person wasn't lucky enough to occupy the front seat of Beto's dilapidation, there was one additional problem he would have to endure. Every rusted-out hole in the floorboard lined up perfectly with a corresponding leak in the exhaust system, so window seats in the front were often fought over.

The morning drives up to the lagoon were never too bad, as it was relatively cool in the pre-dawn hours, and we were always filled with anticipation of that day's fishing. The drive consisted of about fifteen minutes on the paved hibiscus parkways out of Cancun, and then a thirty-minute ass kicking down a rumbly dirt road. Invariably, there was at least one unplanned stop on most mornings, as someone's coffee usually kicked in about ten minutes into the dirt stretch.

The return trips in the afternoon, unfortunately, were a little tougher to bear. You have never experienced the true meaning of the word "funk" until you've shoehorned two sun screened anglers, two sweating Yucatan guides, three gas cans, and a leaking exhaust system into a poorly ventilated van under a blazing tropical sun. One client who fished with Beto on several occasions recalled sharing the back seat with a 150 pound dead jewfish (comida grande).

On most days the round-trip commute was an uneventful success, but on this particular day we were not so lucky.

Bob had caught a couple of baby tarpon that morning, his first with a fly rod, and he was brimming with excitement as he described in great detail each of those experiences while the guides moored the skiffs on the beach and loaded the van for the return drive to Cancun.

"I'll have to say that this is the finest fly-casting trip I've ever been on," he announced as he held up his beer bottle in toast. "Bee-toe, old sport, you run a top drawer operation, here, and I can only hope that tomorrow will be half as good as today."

Beto looked at me and winked, and then he held up his right hand and rubbed his index finger and thumb together like he was caressing a big wad of cash.

The van started up just fine when Beto gave the signal to load and depart, but our troubles began about a mile down the dirt road stretch as Bob was telling Sand Flea about his last trip to Christmas Island. The van didn't sputter, lurch, or cough; it just died quietly and rolled to a stop. We all looked at each other, and then at Beto. He returned our gaze, grinned from beneath his mustache, and uttered that legendary icon of the Latin American dialect, the three words that make every gringo wish he had stayed home and gone trout fishing instead.

"No problemo, amigos!"

"Aaaahhh-jeeeeez...whaaaat-tha hell is going on, here?" Bob whined as Beto hopped out and went around back to open the engine hatch. His mood had switched from unbridled jubilation to absolute despair in less time than it had taken the van's engine to suck in its last breath. "I knew this van wasn't reliable the *minute* I laid eyes on it," he sniveled. "Wait until my travel agent hears about *this!*"

Sand Flea and I bailed out, gasped a breath of fresh air, and went around back with Beto to take stock of our predicament. It was blazing hot, and floating in the cooler were three empty Corona bottles, two crushed Coke cans, a piece of bologna, and a bug-eyed, bloated snapper that Beto had hand-lined out of the mangroves at 7:30 that morning.

If we took off walking we would trek at least two hours in the stifling heat with nothing to drink. My wife had been with me on enough of these trips to know that arrival and departure schedules are seldom reliable. If I wasn't back at the hotel by around 4:30, she would head down to the poolside bar knowing that I would stop there first when I eventually came dragging in. But judging by the way Bob was pacing, and cursing, and wringing his hands, his wife had obviously never been through this one before.

"We've got dinner reservations promptly at six, *BEE-TOE!* So what are the *CHANCES* that this *MACHINE* of yours will get us back to *CANCUN* by that *TIME?*"

Beto, by that point, had already switched his brain into its Selective Understanding of the English Language mode, so he just looked at Bob and shrugged like he had not a clue what the snippy little fella was yammering about. Sand Flea, meanwhile, had found a broken screwdriver under the seat and he had returned to the engine hatch where he was prying and pounding, and singing some snappy little ditty in broken Spanglish.

Knowing that engine repair was not one of my strong suits, I decided to take a seat in the sand under a palm tree and watch the debacle play itself out. At least, for the moment, I was sitting in a relatively cool place where the air wasn't quite so foul.

Finally, after several "chingas" and a couple of "sombeechies" Sand Flea let out a confident "AHH-HAAAH!" He walked to the front, removed an old rusted tackle box from under the seat, and dumped its contents onto the ground. Inside were a couple of corroded hose clamps, a broken spark plug, some blown fuses, a dead scorpion, and a brand new alternator belt still neatly bound together by its cardboard hang tag. I assumed that's what he was looking for when he delicately kissed it, held it aloft, and tongued a few appreciative words to Napacheifautozone, the great Mayan god of van repairs.

"Is that it...is that the problem?" Bob asked as he peered over their shoulders into the engine hatch. Beto turned and looked at Bob. "Shhhhhhhh," he hissed, pointing at Sand Flea as if he were performing brain surgery and needed absolute quiet in the O.R.

Within minutes Sand Flea had replaced the belt, and the van's dead battery with a spare that had miraculously appeared from somewhere behind the back seat. As Beto hopped back into the driver's seat, everyone stood by in eager anticipation as he reached for the ignition. Of course, being the consummate prankster, he cranked his wrist over like he was actually turning the key, and growled, "er-rer-rer-rer-rer." Sand Flea and I thought it was hilarious—as did Beto. Bob was not at all amused. On the next crank the van sprang back to life and Bob's chirpy demeanor and exaggerated Speedy Gonzales accent returned right along with it.

"Si, si—no problemo, amigos! Andele, andele to Cancun!" Beto had obviously saved him from an unspeakable fate by getting that van started again.

With plenty of time to spare, we puttered back into Cancun and dropped Bob off at the Ritz Carlton. His wife was waiting for him near the valet stand, and she too was a bit surprised when her husband stepped out of a van that the hotel groundskeeper wouldn't be caught dead in.

"See you mañana Bee-toe!" Bob waved and yelled as the doorman helped him with his gear, "can't wait to try for that permit!"

"Si mañana—mucho permit," Beto yelled.

As Bob and his wife sashayed back into the Ritz, Beto turned to me and said, "Sand Flea will peek you up mañana, sang time."

"What about Bob?" I asked.

"Bob no fishing, mañana."

"Why not?"

"I'll be seek."

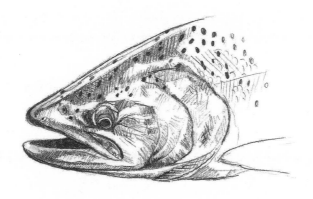

On Bush Pilots

In the mid-90's, Kusko Aviation of Bethel, Alaska was owned and operated by one Fuzzy LaPage. I'm guessing he's probably still there, but when I sat down to write this chapter I decided not to call and check because I knew I'd be disappointed if I found that Fuzzy was no longer flying.

If you wanted to go trout and salmon fishing with Dave Duncan and Sons at one of their Kanketok River tent camps, then you had to sign up with Fuzzy to transport you to and from the river, specifically to a little town on the Bering Sea called Quinhagak. I was never able to master the pronunciation of that town. The natives called it *Kwin-hogggggk* with the latter syllable typically coming forth with a little phlegm behind it.

"Fuzz," as Brad Duncan called him, ran a remarkably tight ship. One of his weekly duties was to drop off the Duncan's anglers each Saturday in Quinhagak and return them to Bethel the following Saturday. He was always on time, and never without a comment or quip about the travel attire, hairstyle, or payload of a Duncan Camp angler. Fuzzy was as predictable as Christmas as long as you stuck to the posted schedule. Stray off the printed page, though, and things might get a little weird.

I met Fuzzy on my first visit to Brad's Lower Base Camp in July of 1995. As usual, I was on one of my multi-lodge tours, so I couldn't spend a full week at any one spot. My hope was to arrive on Tuesday, spend two days on the river, and then depart on Friday. "No problem," said Brad. "Just call Fuzz and he'll take care of you from Bethel out to the camp."

A month later I arrived at the Kusko office at the end of an eighteen-hour travel day. Fuzzy and I exchanged pleasantries; then he weighed my duffel bag, made a remark about the additional baggage around my middle, and asked if I wouldn't mind a couple of "quick stops" along the way.

"Sure," I shrugged, "I'm always up for the scenic route."

He paused, and then he flashed a curious grin; obviously amused by my choice of the word *scenic*. "We'll be ready to roll in about 20 minutes," he said. "Have a seat and help yourself to some coffee."

Sitting in a chair in the loading area was another traveler waiting on a different Kusko departure. He wasn't dressed like a fisherman and I guessed that the greasy Carhartts and black fingernails meant mining or drilling. He was nervous and shifty and after a few minutes he looked my way and asked, "You flown with these guys before?"

"No, you?"

"No. I was supposed to be on a commercial flight to Dillingham but I missed it. Now I gotta fly on one of these wind-ups."

"You don't like small planes?"

"Hate the fuckers."

I chewed on that for a few minutes, and then Fuzzy poked his head in the door and looked toward the nervous guy, "Your pilot's ready."

He got up slowly and I noticed a bead of sweat building on his brow. "Have a good flight," I said.

"I hope so," he managed.

I've never quite understood why some will readily strap themselves into a 300-ton aluminum firecracker and then balk when they're offered a ride in a small plane that actually makes aerodynamic sense. A typical jetliner is held together by miles of wire and hydraulics and its wings are nothing more than glorified rocket fins. One small electrical short can start a catastrophic chain reaction, and when a jet's forward thrust is suddenly arrested it'll drop from the sky like a frozen turkey.

After the nervous guy puttered off toward Dillingham, Fuzzy came back in and gave me the thumbs-up to board. Sharing the ride with a couple of leather-skinned local gentlemen, we loaded up in a little twin-engine and took off over the Kuskokwim River toward a tiny fishing village called Tuntutuliak. There we let off the two elderly men and picked up three very robust Inuit ladies who needed to get to the town of Eek that evening.

"Eek," Fuzzy explained, means "ice" in the local dialect.

He also explained that I was in for a treat because Eek has the shortest runway in Alaska.

A bit later as Eek International airport came into view, I realized why Fuzzy had no hesitation putting three very large people in the back of his plane. We would need all the ballast we could stockpile just to keep from rolling off the runway into the river.

Fuzzy banked in low over the tundra, lined up on the runway, and dropped us in with a landing that could best be described as the old dive-n-skip. I congratulated him on his procedure, but the three ladies in the back didn't seem too impressed. The one wearing camo coveralls with the missing front teeth let out a squeal when her head went *thunk* on the window frame, but there was no comment from the other two.

"That's nothing." Fuzzy boasted, "Wait'l you see me get this plane outa here."

As the ladies said goodbye to Fuzzy, an older man came roaring up the gravel road from town on an old Honda ATV with no fenders. He had a case of muddy lettuce, and he needed to get to Quinhagak, too.

By the time we puttered to the downwind end of the runway, a small crowd of locals had gathered near the tarpaper shack on the bluff overlooking the river. I wondered if perhaps this was their main source of Tuesday evening entertainment.

Fuzzy's about to take off again, better get the boats and some warm blankets ready.

He paused for a moment to check his gauges after pointing the plane's nose into the wind, and then he twisted the throttle forward, released the brakes, and catapulted us down the gravel strip. He didn't even use the whole runway, or even two-thirds of it.

Thirty minutes later we landed in Quinhagak where Brad Duncan was waiting to boat me upriver to his camp. By now I was twenty hours without sleep and notably addled. Fuzz promised to pick me up at noon on Friday, and he assured me that since I was "off-schedule" we'd take the scenic route back to Bethel, as well. He also said that with a few more stops, I'd be eligible for the "Kusko Aviation Frequent Flyer" program.

Brad was impressed with my day of travel. "Wow, you got to land in Eek?" he remarked. "I've been coming up here for fifteen years and I've never landed in Eek."

It was close to 10:00 and Alaska's mid-summer twilight was still two hours away. Big rafts of chum salmon and a few spawning kings were peeling away from our bow wake as we sped upriver, and Brad said there were lots of sore arms and broken rods among the anglers already in camp.

As I sat in Brad's boat pondering the day's events, I wondered why the town of Eek hadn't grown significantly larger over the years. There were no roads across the swampy tundra linking Eek to other settlements; and with a runway that short, Fuzzy could never leave with more people than he brought in.

Note: In the fall of 2003, Alaska said goodbye to one of its finest and most revered bush pilots. Ted Gerken, owner of Iliaska Lodge, lost a valiant battle with cancer, and the fly-fishing community lost an icon of gracious hospitality and fine angling. Aside from giant rainbows on dry flies, Ted and I also shared a passion for bird dogs and shotguns. We chased ptarmigan together on the windswept tundras near his home, and wild bobwhites in the cactus and thornbrush near mine. With Ted it was never about the numbers. He lived and breathed for fine rods, stylish dogs, and properly tuned airplanes. Everything else was incidental.

Big Minnows

My first encounter with tarpon came on a family vacation to Cozumel in the spring of 1980. We were eating dinner at a waterfront restaurant and there was a gang of juveniles hanging out beneath the floodlights and feeding, sporadically, on something that we couldn't quite make out.

When the waiter approached and my dad pointed at the tarpon and asked what they were eating, he glanced over the rail and casually replied, "They are eating the *chit*, señor."

And he was right. They were lurking under the lights, to ambush baitfish like respectable predators should, but they just couldn't pass up those nuggets of incidental protein that were glooping out of the pipe beneath the restaurant bathrooms. Since that day I've chuckled aloud at dozens of different magazine articles that described tarpon as "opportunistic feeders."

I didn't think much about tarpon after the Cozumel incident; like bonefish, though, demand from my traveling clients eventually nudged them to the forefront. I can vividly recall a Friday afternoon in the summer of 1990 when a client dropped by my office with a VHS copy of Billy Pate's *Fly Rodding for Tarpon*. We watched it twice that afternoon and I eventually bought my own copy and played it until it disintegrated.

On the following Monday morning I was on the phone to guides in the Keys, and lodges in Belize, the Yucatan, and Costa Rica. I needed to catch a tarpon, and I needed a slate of quality tarpon destinations for my clients. Bookings and commissions were discussed, dates were arranged, and off I went.

Over the next six years I developed a relationship with tarpon that could best be described as unhealthy. It started in Belize where bad weather turned the fish all pissy and poor execution on my part led to a few fish jumped, but none caught. At Ascension Bay I had a couple of shots but lost the only tarpon I hooked to a flapping loop of line around my rod butt. Later that night I actually got to see a tarpon close up when the bartender at Casa Blanca caught a 20-pounder using a handline made from a Clorox jug, a hundred feet of mono, a rusty hook, and a live pinfish that he snagged beneath the dock lights. In Costa Rica they were rolling in deep muddy rivers and refusing every fly I threw, but a fellow from Birmingham caught a six-footer trolling a big Rapala, and then left it on the dock to rot after posing with it for a picture.

My tarpon miscues continued until I finally caught one in the mangrove lagoons north of Cancun. He was 1/25th the size of the giants that Billy was catching in the video, but at least I got the skunk off the boat.

In the spring of 1992, I finally found an opening with a guide in the Keys, and that's where my tenuous tarpon skills were put under ultimate scrutiny. To that point most of the fish I'd been casting to were juveniles. I'd heard and read plenty about the big Florida migrants but nothing could have prepared me for my first encounter.

It was late May and I was fishing with guide Richard Keating out of Marathon when he poled me up on a gang of adult tarpon off Key Colony Beach. The light was low and they were hanging on the edge of a deep shoal, but still plainly visible. I would later learn that what we saw that morning is known as a "meatball" among the Keys guides. A big school of fish, loitering, slow-rolling, finning, gulping air, happy, willing to eat…a layup, basically.

As Rich poled me closer for an easy downwind shot, I started sweating and my hands got shaky and my Adam's apple began bobbing up and down. When he gave me the nod to cast, I tried to toss the fly to the side and start my windup, but I stepped on a loop of line, botched the load, and ended up with my fly stuck in the rub rail. Rich patiently held me off the approaching school while I cleared the mess, but at that point my calm and confident façade had crumbled in a heap on the bow of his boat. When I finally re-gathered and tried to deliver the fly, it fluttered down within a pile of line about twenty feet shy of the school.

"You're not there, Tosh—try it again…let your line straighten behind you…good…good…now, drop it…no, you're

73

short…go again and load the rod…okay…okay…drop it…still short. Come on Tosh, they're at forty feet…take a deep breath and get it there…nice…niiiiice…nope…still short."

And then the school saw the boat and sank out of view without ever seeing my fly.

For the remainder of that trip, and four more visits to the Keys spanning three seasons, I tried desperately to connect with an adult tarpon. In those days tarpon flies were tied on big hooks, like 3/0 and 4/0, and the patterns hadn't really evolved over quite a number of years. The Florida tarpon were seeing more anglers, with the same flies, and they were increasingly suspicious of them. Often a cast to a string of cruising fish would result in the lead tarpon slamming on the brakes in front of the fly and the followers mounding up behind her like a highway pileup. It was rare to get multiple shots at a pack of happy fish and once they saw the boat they'd duck their heads, string out, and run.

Back then, the old hammer-sweep hookset was the method of choice: a hard yank of the rod opposite the fish's heading, a rotation at the hips, and a sharp jab with the line hand in hopes of driving heavy-gauge steel into a mouth made of bony plates. The hammer-sweep was typically heralded by a guide yelling, "HIT HIM! HIT HIM! HIT HIM!"

Sometimes it worked, a lot of times it didn't. I lost fish because I didn't set quick enough, and others because I set too soon. I broke off a bunch on the hookset, and lost a bunch more on the first head-shake. Getting a big tarpon on the reel in those days was a lot like surviving a lightning strike. One moment you're focused and calm, and then you're connected to a flashing, jolting force that briefly rearranges your protons and neutrons.

With each fishless day I began to press, and the harder I pressed the further I got from landing a tarpon. Between trips I found myself reading every tarpon article and book I could find. I'd think about tarpon in traffic, in church, and while I slept. That overgrown herring had invaded every crevice of my psyche and it eventually took a change of scenery to sort it all out.

In February of 1996, I hosted a group of clients to Belize River Lodge. I'd fished there before, and caught a couple of juvenile tarpon, but there hadn't been much opportunity for adult fish beyond dredging the river mouth with big casting plugs. I brought a 12-weight along, just in case, and was pleasantly surprised when guide Charlie Westby tipped his hand to what he'd found.

"There's a big flat outside, that's got a soft mud bottom," Charlie explained. "We need a calm day to fish it because the wind gets it stirred up. I've been seeing some big tarpon there on nice days. Maybe we'll get lucky."

After three days of wind and marginal fishing in the river, Charlie knocked on the door on the morning of our last day. I was rooming with Ken Houtz, a longtime client from Austin, and he had also expressed interest in trying for big tarpon.

"The wind laid at midnight," Charlie said. "Bring your heavy rods."

We poled around a few mangrove cays early and cast for snook while we waited on the tide change and enough sun to light up the flats.

At 9:30 a.m. Charlie told us to reel up, and when we arrived at the big flat with the muddy bottom, he said, "We've got good sighting. Be ready because it's not a lot of fish. We may only get a few shots."

Ken nodded at me and conceded the bow. "You go first, I've never done this before."

After going through the usual routine of stripping out, casting line, and re-coiling it on the deck, I found myself veiled in a curious calm as we poled across the flat. Maybe I wasn't expecting much, and maybe that's why my knees didn't start knocking when Charlie said, "There's a nice fish just resting there at ten o'clock, about eighty feet. Hold on and let me get you there."

The tarpon was laid up over a patch of turtle grass, a nebulous smear of deep green and chrome. With a couple of silent pushes, Charlie slid the panga within easy range. "Go ahead, Tosh. He's facing a little left, so put the fly about four feet out and a little past his nose."

My cast wasn't great, a little too far outside his view.

"That might work," Charlie said. "Bump it real slow."

When the fly came into view, the tarpon dropped its pectorals, swished its tail and casually fell in line.

"Bump it faster," Charlie whispered. But the tarpon was already committed. With one more tail kick, it rose, opened its big yellow maw, and sucked it in. I was mentally ready for abject chaos, but the fish didn't run at me, or immediately jump, or spit the fly. It made a slow roll to the right, going away, and when my hookset seated the fly in the jaw hinge it accelerated into a long blistering run. Charlie jumped down and stowed his pole, ready

76

to crank the motor if we needed to follow. At about 100 yards the tarpon launched into a series of spectacular greyhounding jumps. Ken was whooping and Charlie was fist-pumping and I was hanging on for dear life.

After about twenty minutes of winding and sweating and tugging, Charlie leaned over the gunnel and grabbed the tarpon's jaw. It was about 6-feet long with a head the size of a small engine block. We took a few photos at boatside, swished some water through its gills, and watched it swim away.

"Congratulations," Charlie beamed and extended his hand.

"That doesn't look so tough," Ken added with a wink.

At 3 p.m. our light tilted upwind and Charlie called it a day. Ken and I had rotated through four big tarpon and I couldn't help but marvel at how calmly he hooked and landed the two that he caught. Beers were pulled from the cooler as Charlie yanked the starter rope and jumped the panga on plane.

"That was the greatest day of fishing I've ever had," Ken said, raising his bottle of Belikin in toast. I clinked his bottle with mine and then turned and raised it toward Charlie.

In August of that year I got a phone call from Ken. "I'll have to cancel my trip back to Belize," he said. "I'm going in for chemo and radiation on Monday. The doctors found a mass in my chest."

Ken died four months later at age 69.

A Matter of Record

My second official brush with angling greatness occurred on a sweltering August morning on the Texas Gulf Coast. It was glassy calm with the humidity at saturation point, and the morning air had all the freshness of a moldy beach towel.

I was looking for redfish, but when I found two acres of tailing black drum in a shallow tidal lake, I remembered my wife's standing request for a few dinner fillets. The drum were spread out over a sandy shoal, five to ten pounders, mostly, and they were plowing up the bottom for crabs, worms, and related morsels.

Black drum fight like the type of dog you'd find under the porch of a crack house, and they're certainly no pushover when it comes to fly selection. It took four fly changes before I found the #6 pearlescent epoxy model they wanted, and I when I finally got it right I doubt they'd have eaten dead shrimp with any less vigor. It was almost automatic: wait for the head on shot, drop the fly in their path, and crawl it along the bottom until they felt it with their barbels.

My plan was to keep three little puppy drum for the stringer, but when I reached that number I still had a hundred yards of sandbar and dozens more fish wagging their tails at me. It was time to experiment.

I switched to a green Clouser. They didn't like it. Poppers, gurglers and sliders? Nope, they wanted nothing to do with surface flies. How about an orange Seaducer? The first pod turned and ran from it, but when I dropped it amongst another advancing troupe my strip met with solid resistance. Oddly, though, there was no drum-like head shaking or bulldogging, and not much running. Just a short dash, a swirl on the surface, and then a series of herky-jerky sprints.

When the mystery fish finally tired and bobbed to the surface, my mouth fell agape when I found a flounder the size of a toilet seat flopping about with my orange Seaducer wedged in its little sidewise mouth. Now, I've never been a cooler-filling consumer of fish, but I will admit to a serious appetite for fresh flounder. They may not be the easiest fish to look at, but damn they're tasty.

With a one-arm bear hug on that night's main course, I quickly untied my stringer and gently removed the third drum. "You should thank Governor Flounder," I told him as he darted away with a small hole in his chin, "he just granted you a stay of execution." The flounder took his place on death row, and without hesitation I turned and high-stepped it back to my boat.

My kids were eating breakfast in front of the TV in a semi-alert trance when I ducked into the kitchen for my fillet knife. They perked up when I told them about the flounder.

"How big is he, Dad?" asked Blake.

"Plenty big. He's down in the boat—come and see."

"How big?" my daughter, Emily, motioned with her hands.

"I didn't weigh him, but he's bigger than Mom's broiler pan."

By the time I found my knife and a Ziploc bag, Blake had plucked the IGFA record book off the shelf and thumbed his way into the Salt Water Fly Rod section.

"Twelve-pound leader?" he asked.

"Yep, I think so."

He studied the listings and then stopped me as I was heading out the door. "Dad, if it's over four pounds you've got a world record!"

"That's an old edition you're looking at, Blake. I'm sure there's been a bigger one caught since then."

I've never been much of a world-record enthusiast. Besides, I had no clue where the nearest certified scale was located and Kathy was already counting on the flounder for dinner that night. Would we do the crab and shrimp stuffing with lemon butter sauce, or charbroiled whole with rice and a big green salad?

The kids came down and studied the flounder just as I was strapping him down on the gurney. "I don't know, Dad," Blake pondered aloud. "Looks pretty big to me. You sure you don't want to send it in for a record?"

Later that afternoon as my headless dinner fish was chilling in the fridge, my curiosity got the best of me so I signed on to the IGFA website and scanned the updated flounder on fly records. Indeed there was a 4-pounder listed under the 12-pound tippet category, but then I noticed that the species heading was for "Summer Flounder." A quick Google search turned up several species of flounder, and the "Summer" variety was described as an East Coast fish. On the Gulf Coast they're classified as "Southern" or "Gulf Flounder." Clicking back to the IGFA site, there was no classification for either species.

How could it be that no southern fly-rodder had ever submitted a flounder on fly? Was it too obscure of a fish? Doubtful; they've got fly-rod listings for Porbeagle Shark and Garrick Leerfish in that book.

A lump formed in my throat. No listings at all for the fish I had just caught. I could've gotten a framed certificate. I could've written a series of articles: Tosh's Tips for Trophy Flounder on Fly. There might've been sponsors and product endorsements. I might've been able to shrink-wrap my entire boat in a beef jerky, smokeless tobacco, or natural male enhancement logo…

Blake was a little chapped that I blew a shot at a world record, but that night's dinner was simply outstanding. He asked before I slid it in the oven if we could still submit it, but I assured him that the IGFA requires the head and body to be intact for a fish to qualify. I knew what he would ask next, so I reminded him that the crabs and catfish on the bottom of the marina had most likely made quick work of the part we threw away.

I mentioned previously that this was my second brush with angling greatness. My first came years before in Port Mansfield when a 19-pound red snapper rose from the depths and plucked my fly from the middle of the chum slick we'd laid out for kingfish. At the time (I learned days later) the red snapper on fly category was also vacant in the IGFA record book.

If my memory serves, we ate that one grilled with new potatoes and a fabulous Veracruz sauce.

Twelve Hours in the Conch Republic

At 6:00 p.m. on the last day of May, a seventeen-year-old matronly tarpon will wander aimlessly into Key West harbor where she will be eternally transformed from a magnificent oceanic migrant into a slovenly dock bum when two kids from Knoxville dump a half-eaten basket of cheese fries and conch fritters in front of the "big-ass whale" as she swims alongside the dock at the Half Shell Raw Bar.

At 5:50 p.m., Dominique and his Flying Housecats will begin setting up their cages, tightropes, ladders, and flaming hoops in the prime performer spot for the evening sunset celebration at Mallory Square while the Romanian guy who can balance a moped on his lips passes by and wonders why his act always gets stuck at the end of the pier next to the guy who sells coconuts with crappy paintings of sailboats and palm trees.

At 5:00 p.m., a pair of twenty-something unwashed skiff guides will finish a Power Bar and Frito dinner after fishing all day and then re-launch their skiffs and motor over to the airport flats to see if they can hit the palolo worm hatch and try a few of the tarpon that their clients couldn't stick with a whaler's lance.

At 4:35 p.m., the biker from Green Bay with the sweaty back pelt will rise from his barstool and grab the South-Beach-looking-guy by the larynx and drag him toward the front door of the Hog's Breath Saloon because he's had his fill of the Miami fan yelling, "Feel-tha-fuckin-HEAT!" as ESPN incessantly replays the previous night's NBA playoff highlights.

Around 4:00 p.m., a sampling of anglers with line-burned fingers and rod-butt bruises on their stomachs will tip their guides and request the exact same dates for next tarpon season while a different sampling of anglers with burned fuses and bruised egos will not tip their guides and mentally tabulate the rate that they've paid per hour to not catch a fish.

At 3:00 p.m., a twelve year old boy from Indiana aboard the Pride of Key West will duck his head in shame and feign anonymity when his father violently sprays his rumen across the Plexiglas and spoils everyone's $28 undersea view of America's only living coral reef.

At 1:30 p.m., an aging fellow from the Bronx with a waggly dewlap and a splotchy sunburn will walk into a water-front clothing store and bray at maximum volume, "*JEEZUS,* who-tha-hell pays, *FIFTY BUCKS* for Sebago sandals?"

At 1:00 p.m., a cruise ship will dock carrying an aging fellow from the Bronx and 1,500 others who are keenly aware of all tolerable price points for resort footwear, fruity libations, and painted coconuts.

At 11:45 a.m., a hundred-pound tarpon in Archer Key Basin will swim away from a skiff towing most of a $90 fly line and the tip section of a $600 rod while an angler steps down from the casting deck to regroup, eat his sandwich, and silently torture himself about the widening gap between the number of tarpon he's jumped in the last four years and the zero tarpon he's landed.

At 10:40 a.m., the driver of the Conch Tour Train will approach the intersection of Truman and Whitehead and line up his little ersatz engine so that all thirty-six tires on the left side of the train will roll over the straw hat with the floral band lying in the middle of the street.

At 10:10 a.m., an obnoxious woman from Schenectady will curse and screech at the driver of the Conch Tour Train when he refuses to stop and retrieve her straw hat with the floral band that one of her own ill-mannered spawn tossed into the street near the intersection of Truman and Whitehead.

Between 8:45 and 10:00 a.m., a dispersion of well-marinated Duval Street patrons will wake up next to people they would have never chosen had they not been swilling fruity libations and slurring campy cover band tunes at 2:00 a.m. on a small island in the neo-tropics.

At 6:45 a.m., an elder guide with ill-conceived notions of seniority will finally get the message that he neither owns nor has grandfathered rights to any flat, basin, or shoal in the Florida Keys when he opens his hatch and finds the putrid severed head of a jack crevalle resting atop his brand-new rain jacket.

At 6:00 a.m., a thousand tarpon (minus one) that are scattered between the Pearl Basin and the Marquesas will stop loitering and resume migrating when they sense the initial gravitational tug of the three-quarter moon and the first hint of the morning flood tide.

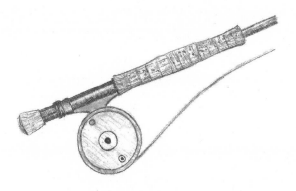

You've Got Mail!

The letters all arrived within the same week. Just three years after the internet became mainstream, the "Big Three" airlines decided that travel agents, and the commissions they earned, were no longer necessary. I knew it was coming, as they'd been trimming commissions for several months, but I didn't expect the dominoes to tumble en masse.

The actual wording varied between American, Delta, and United, but their message in the spring of 1999 was essentially the same: due to our increasing capability to book passengers directly through our websites, we are no longer paying commissions to travel agents. Within two days the same letter began arriving from the smaller carriers.

At that point my little sporting travel agency was sending clients to about sixty lodges and outfitters from Alaska to Argentina. While the lodge commissions were generous, the airline income was a significant percentage of our bottom line. Not only were we booking the flights for our clients to fish and hunt abroad, we were also booking many of their family vacations and business trips.

With two young kids at home needing more of my time, I was thinking of hiring a couple of associates to help me expand the business and reduce my travel time. Those plans were immediately shelved and within a few weeks it became apparent that I was stuck between the veritable rock and the actual hard place; a huge reduction of income meant not enough capital to hire, and the inability to hire meant more time away from my family. The cruise lines were still paying a cut to travel agencies, but I'd never heard of anyone catching a fish off Carnival's Pathogen of the Seas.

For the second time in our relationship I had to bounce a career change off Kathy, and for the second time she asked, "What is it that you *really* like to do?"

"Well, I *still* really like to hunt and fish, but I've also got thousands of 35mm slides that I've shot from around the world, so maybe I'll send a few out and see what they're worth?" An old website came down, a new website went up, and a month later I sold my first magazine cover. Al Gore's internet had killed one business and enabled another.

Onward.

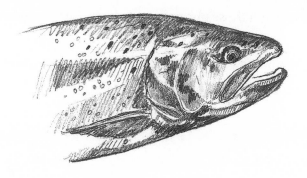

The Deke

Flowing water has a sanctimonious way of pre-qualifying its clientele. Gentle riffles and wide gravel bars lure the false-casting masses, while boiling black holes rimmed with mossy ledgerock frighten them away.

That said, I suppose there's really no great mystery why the easy flows produce the fussy little degree-candidate fish, while the spiteful, intimidating rivers hide the big gluttonous thugs.

British Columbia's Babine River had been high on my list for quite some time and I jumped at the opportunity when I heard that a prime space had opened up in October of 2001. I didn't have any steelhead images in my stock files and demand for those photos was fairly high.

"Big steelhead, but not an easy river to fish." I was told by outfitter, Tom Knopik, who had fished the Babine many times. Naturally, I spun those phrases around in my mind for a few days and then conveniently extracted the words easy, big, and steelhead. Six months later I would fully realize the significance of that mistake.

On my first run downriver from Norlakes Lodge, I noticed that my guide, Darcy Edwards, seemed most interested in stretches of water that an adult moose wouldn't try to cross. Darcy would slow down and peer intently into the deep, rolling holes, and then he'd rev up his throttle and race top-speed through the slower, shallow runs.

"That's a good looking pool," I cautiously announced as we turned a corner and sped through a long glassy flat with a nice riffle at the top.

"Dickwater," Darcy scoffed, "there ain't no steelhead in that."

After passing a few more of those placid runs, we finally stopped along a steep shoreline littered with fallen spruce trees where Darcy pointed among the blow-downs into a cauldron of crashing water. "This here's where you're gonna spank their scaly asses," he announced, "Grab the rod with your heaviest sinking line and hop on out."

He was about to shove off and check on another angler downstream when he noticed me standing on the bank and staring at the river like an overwhelmed toddler.

"How should I fish this?" I inquired with as little poise as I could manage.

"Wade deep and cast far," he shouted over the drone of his

outboard. Fortunately, he noticed my look of complete unease at that point, so he tossed his anchor back onto the rocks and offered a bit more advice.

"See that big boiler out there in the middle," he pointed to an exposed rock the size of a Toyota that was dividing the flow into two raging currents, "the deke is just in front of it and behind it."

"The what?"

"The deke."

"What the hell's a *deke*?"

"It's the sweet spot, the place where the steelhead like to hold."

"Okay. No problem on that deke part, but can I try it from the other side of the river?

"What for?"

"There's no room for a backcast here?"

He was crimping down the barb on a big, gaudy string-leech, and he paused and squinted from beneath his hat brim. "Can't you roll cast?"

"I can roll cast a dry line, but not a full-sink."

Darcy casually reached for my rod and plunged out into the torrent to the upper limit of his waders. He then stripped off about sixty feet of line, looped it into five big coils, flipped the lead-core and the fly into the current, and skated it back to the top. With the tip pointing skyward, he paused briefly to load the rod, and then with one seamless downstroke he fluently rolled and fired the entire line across the river. "It's all about timing," he shrugged. "The less effort you put into it the better."

The cast, itself, was remarkable. The fly landing perfectly on target and sweeping right through the deke was even more impressive. Most astonishing, though, was Darcy managing the entire gymnastic display without losing the inch-long ash that was dangling off the tip of his cigarette.

Since I just stood there dumbfounded, Darcy assumed that I had a full grasp of the concept, so he hopped back in the boat and blasted off downriver.

Two hours later I was still standing in the same spot, but despite several hundred attempts to replicate Darcy's roll cast, my fly hadn't landed within a cannon shot of that sorry ass deke.

When Darcy finally returned to check my progress, he found me halfway up the bank trying to tear down a spruce tree that held my fly. He killed his motor and sat watching me for a moment before making an intuitive assumption.

"Roll cast ain't quite workin', eh?"

I shook my head, no.

"Catch anything?"

"This tree, four times."

Sensing my exasperation, Darcy took me downriver to a nice little run with a long gravel bar and plenty of room for a backcast. There was a current seam at the head of the pool that even I could recognize, and there was one addlepated steelhead holding in the middle of it. We worked on my roll cast for a while after releasing the fish, and then we took a lunch break as the clouds lowered and a cold, steady rain moved in from the west.

"Ya like that run?" Darcy asked through a mouthful of soggy sandwich.

"Yep. Nice to wade, easy to cast."

"Well that's good," he said as he packed away his lunchbox and yanked the starter rope on the outboard. "I'm glad we got your confidence up, 'cause you're gonna spend the afternoon at a nice little spot called Roll Caster's Hell."

By the fourth day of our trip I had perfected something that behaved a bit like a roll cast; but according to the trained observers in my party, my version more closely resembled someone trying to hack vines out of a tree with a fly rod. I did manage a semi-respectable fish tally by week's end, but more important than my number of actual steelhead hookups, I left the Babine with a whole cache of new experiences.

In twenty-five years of fly-fishing, I had never before lived that moment of gasping, flailing panic when the current deftly removes your feet from the bottom and fills your carefully layered wader/garment ensemble with forty-degree water.

I had never gone through three dozen flies and thirty yards of leader material in a single week of fishing, nor had I ever lost both a fly line and a very pricey drag system to a single fish.

On this trip I met a freshwater sociopath capable of melting a line crease into my stripping finger, and in that same specie I found a picky bastard requiring more casts per bite than the lowly snook. A snook eats a fly because it occasionally gets hungry; a steelhead occasionally eats a fly because it's a passive-aggressive manipulator of men.

This game is not for the delicately wired sport who requires constant action as the measure of a good fishing trip. It's a lonely and punishing grind; a meticulous regimen of cast, mend, swing it slow, step down…cast, mend, swing it slow, step down. If you don't catch a fish on the first pass through a good run, change flies and go through it again. Lather, rinse, repeat.

And don't bother trying to re-focus after your mind has wandered and you can't remember your last dozen casts. You won't get an eat when you're expecting one—especially after you've made a cast of which you're particularly proud. If two fish on the Babine is a good day, and a six fish day is off the charts, then it doesn't take a math scholar to deduce the average number of hours between bites.

Incidentally, I found that singing and humming can pass the time quite nicely between sporadic steelhead events, especially if you can come up with a song that'll torment your subconscious for the entire week…

> *And ev-ery one was an (H)en-er-y*
> *She never had a Willie or a Sam*
> *I'm her eighth ole man; I'm (H)en-er-y*
> *(H)en-er-y the Eighth, I am*

Sometimes the eventual strike is just a subtle tick at the bottom of your swing, or it might be a slow tightening of your line that feels no different from the dozens of rocks and logs you've been snagging. But then comes the big grab, the one that reminds you why you signed up for steelhead in the first place. A strike so savage that you finally understand why your guide keeps telling you to quit trout fishing and get rid of that loop of slack line before something bad happens.

Even though this fish offers one of the greatest fly rod challenges in fresh water, I am not a hopeless steelhead addict, nor will I ever become one. The best steelheading happens during the fall and so do many of my other rod and gun vices. Sure, I'll go again someday, and when I do I'll probably go back to the Babine. I've got too much invested in long underwear and bulletproof waders to go anywhere else, and fishing a more forgiving river would be like regressing to the bunny slopes after winning the giant slalom.

From a popularity perspective, one can only assume that the passing of seasons won't be too much for a river as merciless as the Babine. She's a long way from anywhere, and even if a new crowd of people put forth the effort every year, only a fraction of them will fall under her spell. Even if you love the Babine, she can still be a river that you love to hate.

But regardless of my return date, be it sooner or later, I have borrowed a small piece of the Babine experience that I'll carry with me wherever I fish.

It might be that single impulsive bonefish on the edge of the pack that's grubbing the bottom a little harder than the others, or maybe it's the feeding, tailing permit instead of the indifferent cruiser. Perhaps it's the fifth tarpon back in the string, the spontaneous follower instead of the suspicious bell cow in the lead.

There's always a deke.

Try to hit it.

Fishanoma

I am a white man. Not just categorically white; I mean physically white. Fair-skinned and freckled. As a point of reference, if Nicole Kidman and I were to marry and start a family, our children would be born translucent.

Foolishly, I believed growing up that one day I'd accumulate enough UV rays to meld my freckles together and permanently change my skin tone. But after four decades of reckless pan-frying, I've still got no more pigmentation than the average garden grub.

I was in my late twenties when skin cancer started getting lots of press. Mildly concerned, but not quite scared, I began buying sunscreen and going through the motions. I'd dab a little here and there before each day of fishing and then return to the dock ten hours later with my ears sizzling like sausage patties.

White, mottled red, then back to white again. That process repeated itself time and again until February 2002 when the skin cancer topic finally hit closer to home.

I was at the boat ramp on Sugarloaf Key with Albert Ponzoa when he got the dreaded phone call from his doctor.

"Albert, how long did you say that spot's been on your lip?"

"About a month, why?"

"You're tests came back positive. You've got squamous cell carcinoma."

"Dammit."

Albert had always worn a facemask, sunscreen, and long sleeves since I had known him as a guide, but he admitted that years of unprotected swimming and fishing during his childhood had obviously caught up with him.

A few days later I was back home in Austin awaiting my first-ever dermatological exam, while Albert was having his lower lip torched away in Miami. Unfortunately, Bill Ramsdell, the (avid fisherman) dermatologist that I had hoped to see was booked up for months, so I scrambled through the phone book and found another doctor with a quick opening. I was nervous going in and scared stiff when I came out.

She was pallid, condescending, and abrupt with wiry black hair and no apparent sense of humor. When she glared contemptuously over the rim of her glasses, she reminded me of my second grade teacher in a lab coat.

She started by asking lots of questions about my history of sun exposure, all the while frowning, wincing, and saying

100

things like "hmmm," "ouch," and "I see." I explained that my work required a substantial number of days in the sun each year, but judging by the intensity of her scowl, I decided to leave out the number of personal fishing days.

When the interview was over, she meticulously inspected every inch of my body (even though I reminded her that jail terms are typically assigned to people who fish naked) and then she proceeded to lecture, scold, and browbeat me about my irresponsibility. She froze a scabby-looking thing off my earlobe, razored two moles off my back, and then sent me home with a stack of brochures and pamphlets for prescription sunscreen, big goofy hats, and UV-safe clothing. A few days later I learned that none of the things she removed were malignant, but she was quick to point out that I was darn lucky to have gotten away with just a couple of small scars.

"What about my work?" I asked her one more time.

"That's up to you," she snapped, "but with your fair skin I'd consider another profession."

I thought about that suggestion for a few days, and I also considered Albert's predicament. His surgery had been a success. The cancer hadn't spread to his lymph system, and he was back on the water a couple of weeks later. Same program as before: bandanas, long sleeves, and lots of sunscreen. He wasn't giving up guiding, and he's out in the sun tenfold more days than me.

Ha! I'll show her!

For the next year or so I experimented with several preventative programs. Switching to long sleeves and wearing a facemask was no problem, but I live in the south and wear shorts nine months of the year. Fishing in long pants during the summer swamp-ass season was simply not an option.

What I eventually found after considerable trial and error was that dressing for comfort and frequent sunscreen applications would maybe keep me somewhat cancer free. That program would buy me time on the water, I reasoned, but for absolute peace of mind I decided to take it a step further.

After waiting patiently for an open appointment slot with Dr. Bill, I became an official member of his frequent freezing program. Twice per year, or whenever something scaly or suspicious emerges on my dermis, I drop in to see him for a thorough screening and a quick recap of recent fishing trips. When the fish talk is over he pulls out his penlight, pokes at a couple of moles, and never asks me to drop my shorts. "We need to stay on top of these little pre-cancer spots on your scalp," he says. And with that he whips out his little ice-torch and hits me with a couple of quick blasts.

Then we're done. No scolding and no guilt trips. Sure, I'll walk around for a day or two looking like Nuclear Accident Man, but then the freezer-burned patches begin sloughing away and I'm good to go for another six months.

Now, granted, what's good for me might not work as well for you, so please don't announce to your dermatologist that I said it's okay to fish your way around the equator in a Speedo. And please don't underestimate my newfound diligence for applying sunscreen. If Coppertone Sport SPF 48 came in 50-gallon drums, I'd be wheeling it out of my local Walgreens on a hand-truck.

There's a fairly prevalent history of cancer in my family,

and I'm acutely aware of the risk of too much sun exposure. But, I'm also a believer that cowering like a salamander in a cool, dark place and thereby depriving yourself of fish, water, and sunny skies is potentially just as damaging as a UV overdose.

Lather up, get outdoors, and cast a line. And if your nose gets a little crispy, then go find a dermatologist with fishing magazines in his waiting room.

Bite or Be Bitten

Our approach spooked a pair of squawking scarlet macaws when we motored in. It was a small lagoon surrounded by a hundred-foot tree canopy and an exposed sandbar along the far shore. My guide, Haroldo, cut the outboard and quietly picked up his paddle. As we approached the sandbar a shower of sardinatas erupted from the shallows with a gang of hoodlums in pursuit.

They were juvenile peacock bass and they had the school of food exactly where they wanted them. My line came tight after a couple of noisy chugs with a pencil popper and when Haroldo leadered the peacock and swung it into the boat, a small sardinata flopped out of its mouth onto the deck.

"Damn…a brook trout wouldn't last five minutes in this river," I remarked as Haroldo leaned over the gunnel to wash the slime off his hands. "He'd get ripped to shreds before he ever noticed the heat."

Haroldo looked up and smiled, and then he nodded like Brazilian fishing guides typically do after pauses in conversation that might indicate the end of a sentence.

"You believe in natural selection?" I asked.

Another brief smile, followed by a blank stare.

"You know...Charles Darwin...survival of the fittest?"

"...eh?"

"Never mind."

On the next cast I caught a beautiful little butterfly peacock; lime green with three black and gold haloed spots on its flank. Haroldo was digging in the cooler for his water bottle when I opened its chops to remove the fly and found a horrifying little creature attached to its tongue.

"*Jesus*! What is *that* thing?"

He sprang to his feet and peered down the fish's maw as I held it open with my forceps. "Es no bad," he replied as he whipped out his Leatherman and reached in to dislodge the creature. He placed the six-legged maggot on his palm and studied it for a moment, and then he turned and booger-flicked it into the river.

"No good to eat?" I asked, making the universally accepted hand-to-mouth gesture.

"Nah. No eat," he laughed, with a slight hint of *you igno-rant gringo* in his expression.

The little peacock had two red pincer marks on its tongue, but otherwise it appeared to be fine. "You're welcome," I said to the fish after I placed it back in the water and watched it dart away from the boat.

"Big peacock...we go?" Haroldo asked with his hands spread about four feet apart. He was obviously hoping that I'd become bored catching fish that generate small tips. I shrugged and nodded as he lifted the trolling motor and fired up the outboard.

We sped along through a maze of flooded jungle off the Rio Jatapu's main course and then stopped next to a broad flat with standing trees in about fifteen feet of water. Haroldo jumped up to the bow, grabbed a casting rod with a hookless Woodchopper plug, and began plowing the coffee-colored water in hopes of raising a big fish. I prudently followed each cast with a streamer fly that looked like a flaccid toucan, but after several dozen attempts our bait-and-switch program failed to provoke the thick-skulled bruiser we were after.

I assumed we were quitting for lunch when Haroldo stowed the Woodchopper and mumbled something I couldn't understand; but he perked up again when my streamer suddenly disappeared in a splashy boil next to the boat. It wasn't the peacock bass we were after, but I would soon learn exactly how Haroldo felt about piranhas.

"Ahh-haaaaa! Pee-ran-ya!" he sneered, as he grabbed the net and motioned excitedly for me to steer the thrashing demon his direction. He waited for the snapping and flopping to subside, and then he carefully wrapped his hand around my leader and hoisted the fish from the mesh. I had turned to reach for my camera, and I was stunned when I saw the flash of steel and the splatter of blood on the deck. With the precision and pageantry of a Japanese fry-cook, Haroldo had sliced the piranha's tail off and quickly returned it to the river—still firmly attached to the end of my line. I wasn't quite sure what he hoped to accomplish as the hapless piranha flopped and bled on the surface, but then its schoolmates rose from the depths and immediately hacked it into a slimy froth.

Even though I hadn't noticed any pockmarks or missing toes, this young Brazilian had obviously had an unpleasant piranha experience at some point in his life.

He let go with a sadistic cackle as the last of the piranha scraps were plucked from the surface, and then he clapped his hands and pumped his fist in the air as the bloodstain faded away in the river. When I stripped my fly back to the boat after the execution was over, I found only a bare hook with a couple of hackle fibers and a small piece of piranha lip clinging to the barb.

"Just like in the movies, Haroldo."

[Broad smile]

"I guess tadpoles and crappie never gained much of a foothold in the Amazon?"

[Blank stare]

Out of curiosity, I flicked what was left of my streamer back in the river and it was immediately inhaled by another piranha. This time, using hand gestures, body language and all the Portuguese I could manage, I explained to Haroldo that affluent sporting magazines back home will pay huge license fees for shots of exotic jungle sport fish. I promised him a healthy percentage of the take if he'd hold it up just long enough for a photo.

He agreed, and instead of immediately sacrificing this one after the photo session, he turned and tossed it into the live well.

A few days later, I was checking in at the Varig Airlines counter in Manaus when the security gal unzipped my rod case and noticed a suspicious parcel of paper towels tucked discreetly inside the tube. As a waft of nastiness escaped from the case and assaulted her sinuses, she summoned her co-workers, pulled on latex gloves, and gingerly unrolled the boiled, toothy skull that was wrapped within.

"Ooooooooh...pee-ran-ya?" she asked, still waving her hand in front of her crinkled nose.

I nodded and smiled like a typical unknowing American, hoping they wouldn't confiscate the odiferous curio that I intended to smuggle home through US Customs. By now a small crowd of uniforms and badges had gathered and all progress in the inspection line had ground to a halt. The security officers were eyeing me intently and sniffing around my rod case like a pack of meerkats when a mustachioed gentleman stepped forward and pointed suspiciously at my prized souvenir.

"You have eaten the pee-ran-ya?" he asked (using the universally accepted hand-to-mouth gesture).

Hoping to avert a comprehensive luggage search for frozen piranha fillets, I looked him straight in the eye and told him exactly what he needed to hear. He turned and spoke to the rest of the security staff and then motioned for me to continue through the line.

"What did he say?" I asked the gal who had first opened my rod case.

With a broad smile she replied, "He says you are free to board and the Americans can keep the skull and put you in jail when you arrive in Miami."

Note: I later found that the parasitic alien attached to the peacock bass tongue is one of many isopods from the Cymothoidae family. They enter a host fish through the gills and attach themselves to its tongue. Over time they will actually drain the tongue of blood and digest it. From there they remain attached and the shape of their carapace serves as a replacement to the fish's tongue. The fish typically survives and can continue to feed without issue and the transient gets a few bites of every meal. Is that crazy, or what?

Extremes

Mired in the crumbling south bank of the Brownsville Ship Channel was a derelict destroyer of World War II vintage. Her name was sandblasted from her bow and she was listing heavily to port. Jagged windows had been torched through her hull to keep the welders from slow-roasting inside her belly while they systematically reduced her down to scrap iron. On my left, on the north shore of the channel, was a sprawling ghetto of head-high weeds, rusting shrimp boats, jack-up rigs, and industrial detritus. There were no people around and I wondered if anyone would care if I found something in the heap with a live battery and drove off with it.

My friend, Dale Fridy, and I went there to catch a snook. It was calm and foggy when we arrived at dawn and a six-incher ate my fly on the first cast. We saw bigger ones but they wouldn't eat because snook are fastidious little pricks, even in Texas. At 9:00 a.m. a broiling hot wind kicked up from the southwest. After a number of attempts to hold us within casting range of the likely snook holds (submerged tractor tires and cable spools) Dale turned and looked my way with an exasperated shrug.

"I'm not sure I'm as motivated at this point as I was two hours ago," I told him. We had found big pods of tailing redfish under gulls the day before, and we both knew the snook deal was a mission of whimsy, at best.

"Too bad they don't live in a prettier place," he remarked as we turned toward Port Isabel and jumped up on plane.

Snook are making a slow comeback on the lower Texas coast but it's only a matter of time before another killer freeze halts their progress. The last one was in February of 1989 when the shallow flats actually crusted over with an icy salt slush and the coons, crabs, and seagulls gorged on the resulting fish kill.

We live at the northern fringe of the snook's acceptable range; that's the standard excuse we all trumpet whenever it's more convenient to avoid the topics of habitat mismanagement and environmental idiocy. The acceptable range theory doesn't explain, though, why fifty years ago they thrived as far north as Port O'Connor and grew so big they were ugly. They disappeared about the same time the great Texas tarpon migration halted.

As we motored back toward the dock, the wind blowing across the channel had stirred up a significant chop and every third wave was breaking over Dale's skiff deck and blasting us in the face. Between the snook hole and Port Isabel, the Brownsville Ship Channel cuts through several thousand acres of barren sand and salt flats. It hadn't rained in South Texas in months and when we reached the cut through the flats we found a mile-wide curtain of dust blocking the sun and blowing across the channel. Were we not running balls-out in a sixteen foot-poling skiff you could have easily painted us into one of those embedded CNN broadcast scenes from Iraq.

On the other side of the dust cloud we found three-foot rollers at the channel mouth so Dale angled his bow at the troughs and we took a few more waves in the face to wash away the grime. Most evidence of the dust storm was gone when we arrived back at the ramp, except for the mud between my teeth and a dripping reddish glob in Dale's right ear. We parted ways at the dock and promised to meet up again if we could make an impromptu match of calm weather and an opening in his date book.

At that point, I was a four-hour drive from Port Aransas and the next day's photo shoot. It was just shy of noon, the wind was still roaring like a blast furnace, and the thermometer in my truck read 94 degrees.

After leaving the Rio Grande Valley, Texas Highway 77 cuts a sixty-mile swath northward through the heart of the King Ranch. During wet springs this desolate stretch is lush and vibrant with standing water, wildflowers, waist-high grass, and butterflies bouncing off the windshield.

But this year the King Ranch was a parched moonscape of blowing sand and withered prickly pear. Unfortunately, they were due for a protracted dry spell. It rained buckets there in 2004-05 and it's an accepted fact in Texas that no ranch will ever get more than two wet years in a row. South Texas rangeland can recover quickly from a drought; all it takes is a few successive soaking rains.

Our estuarine bay systems, unfortunately, tend to languish and suffer a bit longer. Without significant freshwater inflow the bays and flats become hyper-saline and the propagation of crabs, shrimp, and baitfish suffer terribly. No forage fish, no gamefish.

When I reached the old Armstrong rail stop the thermometer on my truck mirror read 104. A half hour later as I approached the Border Patrol checkpoint at Sarita, the LED readout jumped from 106 to 109. There was a small grass fire between the north and southbound highway lanes and a crew of State workers was trying to keep it confined to the median. The checkpoint was choked with acrid, blowing smoke, and a half-dozen turkey vultures were perched in the mesquites and waiting to pounce on anything smoldering and crispy left exposed on the charred ground.

In front of me in the checkpoint line was a pickup with an elegantly scripted rear window sticker announcing that *Arturo y Isabella* were the occupants and likely owners. In the back of their truck was a sparsely-haired piebald dog tethered between a twin mattress and a Kenmore washer-dryer combo.

Border Patrol agent "Sanchez" was standing on asphalt that was undoubtedly much hotter than the air temperature. His shoes were sticking and squishing in the hot mix as he stepped forward to inspect each arriving vehicle. He was dripping with sweat and I'm pretty sure he hated his job. His drug-sniffing

German Shepherd was asleep in the shade next to the checkpoint office. Without a word of interrogation, and barely a glance inside their vehicle, he waved *Arturo y Isabella* through the checkpoint.

"Did you know it's a hundred and nine damn degrees?" I asked when I idled up to his post. He didn't answer, nor did he seem to appreciate the blast of air conditioning that escaped when I rolled down my window. He scowled and waved me through without a word, and he did the same with the Ramirez Quality Produce truck waiting in line behind me.

I wondered if he badgered Dick Cheney's entourage with questions when they rushed through this same checkpoint four months ago with a bird-shot attorney in the back of their black Suburban.

Homeland Security.

When I reached Kingsville the mercury dipped back to 107, and I turned on my weather radio when I noticed a thin line of demarcation building in the overheated sky. There were significant buildups to the north and west of Corpus Christi ahead of a cool front that was spilling down through the Texas Hill Country. The entire Coastal Bend and all counties to the south were under a severe thunderstorm watch for the remainder of the evening.

It was 97 degrees when I reached Robstown. The wind had stopped blowing and the sky was chalky white. When I climbed the hump on the Kennedy Causeway heading toward Mustang Island, the sky over Corpus Christi Bay was blackish blue and streaked with lighting; 89 degrees. The first raindrops splattered my windshield as I pulled into Port Aransas. The wind was now gusting from the north; it was 76 degrees and the day-glow painted foam seahorses were bucking and swaying on their poles in front of the souvenir shop at the corner of Alister and the Cutoff Road.

For the next two hours I sat on the balcony watching an exceptional orchestration of rain, lighting, and waves crashing on the bulkhead. When I left Port Isabel at noon, I would have never thought that a jacket might be necessary at some point on this particular day.

At 7:15 p.m. the Island Queen party boat motored out of Port Aransas harbor and headed toward the jetties. It was still raining and blowing and it appeared that there were only two paying customers on board. They were standing near the bow, undaunted, with a bundle of bottom-fishing rods propped next to them on the rail. If the waves rolling across the pass from the north were three-feet high, then I can't imagine how big they were out at the jetties where these sports were headed. If not *now*, then at what point *does* an operator of bargain fishing tours decide that it's not worth going out?

The watches and warnings finally expired around 9:30 p.m. and the late newscast in Corpus Christi presented a half-hour account of wind damage, street flooding, and hail the size of snowcones.

A man in Flour Bluff described the sound of a tornado to the roving reporter wearing a rain slicker. He couldn't confirm on camera that he actually saw it, but it rolled his boat and trailer down the street and he said that it didn't sound like a hurricane because he'd "rode out three of those."

The weatherman was so excited about the day's events

that he forgot to provide anything resembling a forecast for the next day.

Before my alarm went off, I was nudged awake by the north wind whistling around the bedroom window frame. Out front the waves were still crashing into the bulkhead. The NOAA site confirmed a small craft advisory for the rest of the day so I tossed my camera box and duffel into the truck for the drive back to Austin.

As I sat in the ferry line with a cup of coffee watching the muddy combers running down the ship channel, my truck mirror displayed 59 degrees. The morning radio newscaster in Corpus Christi proudly proclaimed that we had all just witnessed an historic weather event. The 3.89 inches of rain that fell the afternoon before ended their longest spring dry spell in twenty years. It was also the largest single day rainfall ever recorded in the month of May. In addition, the official high temperature of 104 just before the frontal passage was the hottest ever recorded in the month of May.

"So folks," announced the radio weather man, "May 10th, 2006, will officially go down as the driest, hottest, and wettest twelve hour period we've ever seen."

Some researchers say that the bizarre weather we've experienced over the past few years is a cyclical thing that will average out over time. Others claim that we've officially breached our environmental contract with planet Earth and we've only seen a preview of the weirdness to come.

Will there be more extended droughts in South Texas? Yes, you can count on that one; nothing really weird, there. Will

Port Aransas ever see another three-inch snowfall like they had Christmas morning 2004? Doubtful, but after yesterday's fifty-degree temperature swing I wouldn't completely rule it out. How about yet another summer without a catastrophic hurricane leveling a major Texas seaport?

It's been twenty-four years since the last costly hit (Alicia, Galveston, two billion), and our 375 mile coastline is shaped like a giant catcher's mitt. If I may broaden the baseball metaphor: we're now in the bottom of the ninth, down by two, with two outs, and no runners on base.

But a bigger question remains: Will I one day find scads of snook lounging around on a sparkling south Texas grass flat like they presumably did fifty years ago? In the news, these days, we find increasing reports of tropical species found far north of where they typically hang out. Will we ever find bonefish on the Louisiana Delta?

If so, you can bet that approximately half of this country will either blame or credit their arrival on whomever lives in the White House at the time.

Note: On September 13, 2008 Hurricane Ike rolled in just east of Galveston and racked up 20 billion in damage. In metaphorical baseball, Ike was a walk-off homer.

Gentlemen of The Angle

The Been There Done That Guy

He is a walking, burbling authority on guides, lodges, rivers, oceans, lakes and fish. He's the best caster he's ever met. He sets up his vise in the middle of the bar during happy hour and forces you to notice his extraordinary tying skills. He owns three obscure IGFA records and is working on six more that no one will care about. He'll ask you a question about fishing just so he can cut you off in mid-reply and answer it himself. He is the most uninteresting man in the world.

The Industry Guy

He comes in many forms: shop owner, travel agent, writer, photographer and gear rep. If he's a new industry guy he'll do well to keep his voice down and his head below the radar. If he's a career industry guy he'll concede the best guides, sleep in the worst bed, eat leftovers with the kitchen help, and repeatedly announce to everyone within earshot, "I'm just happy to be here!"

The Finagler

If you're sharing the lodge with this guy, you should take comfort in the fact that you're booked into the absolute best week of the year for wind, sunlight, tide, temperature, moon phase, barometric pressure, and solunar peaks. He wouldn't be there if all those planets weren't perfectly aligned. Unfortunately, your week will still suck because he has left you with the worst guide, a leaky boat, last choice of fishing water, and a room with a small insect problem.

The Gear Queer

You know him well. He ships his rod and duffel armory to the lodge a week in advance. He cleans his fly lines at the top of each hour and replaces his backing nightly. He can tie knots blindfolded that Flip and Lefty have never heard of. He never picks up a fly rod without wiggling the tip and then pausing with furrowed brow to deeply contemplate something about its design that doesn't really matter. His leader recipes are written on laminated index cards. His fishing vest is a bulging, tangled grab bag of useless doohickeys. He firmly believes that the next great rod design is the one that will finally allow him to accurately deliver a fly past his current maximum range of twenty-six feet.

The Life of the Party

He's the last one to bed and the last one up. If he gets on the water at all it's only because the lodge bar is closed during fishing hours. Sometimes he'll have a trophy companion in tow. If she's still on her feet after happy hour and dinner, there's a good chance that the lodge's weekly tip pool will be quickly depleted in $1 increments.

The Whiner

Hold your nose while reading this aloud and exaggerate each syllable break. My bed sheets are gritty. My guide called me a Pendejo. Our motor runs really smoky. Two bath towels for an entire week? These fish are really spooky. Does the wind always blow this hard? There's a scorpion in my shower. I've only caught two fish all week. Twenty bucks a day for guide tips? The lettuce on my sandwich is wilted. Do you have any Dijonnaise?

The Angler

This is the guy that you likely didn't notice. He brought the right gear and knew how to use it. He caught plenty of fish, but didn't feel the need to tell you about each of them. He was the nice guy at the dinner table that listened more than he talked; the guy who's face you'll probably remember, but whose name you'll never recall.

Pilot Error

Like all proper and complete travel memoirs, this one has a beginning, middle, and end. But, since this recollection is about the Bahamas—specifically my traveling *within* the Bahamas—the middle portion is significantly less interesting than the rest.

Having fished a number of Bahamian islands over the years, I've noticed an inclination, of sorts, in the way those trips typically play out. On the front end there will be a travel day (or two) that might involve a fair amount of consternation and perhaps gnashing of teeth. This is especially true if along the way you switch from a U.S. carrier to Bahamasair. In the middle of the trip there will typically be fair weather, exciting fish, conch fritters, beautiful waters, and cheerful accommodating locals. On the back end, unfortunately, there will be another travel day (or two).

If your outbound leg progresses smoothly, you should prepare yourself for an all-inclusive beat down of your mental and physical being on the return trip; I'm almost certain that someone is keeping track.

Now that you've been briefed on my opinion of flying certain airlines in the Bahamas, I give you the events of April 10, 2007.

Nassau is hot and crowded and only marginally appealing when I arrive there at 4:30 p.m. from DFW. On my left, as my taxi noses along through traffic that reminds me of home, is a periodic view between buildings and down alleyways of the massive Atlantis Resort and Casino complex. It's tall and shiny and garish and no doubt responsible for the ambitious room rates at even the seediest hotels on this island.

Out my right side window is a stop-and-start-inch-along-block-by-block view of downtown Nassau. I'm sure it would look better at a faster rate of progress, but as we trundle along at a conch-like pace I'm noticing that most buildings need a fresh coat of paint to disguise their thirty years of deferred maintenance.

On this particular afternoon, I am a number of things: I'm forty-three, and I'm tired, and I'm overdressed because it was cold when I left home this morning. So, now I'm hot, and therefore I smell.

Today, though, in downtown Nassau, as my taxi edges past the courthouse and past the assemblage of news trucks and reality rubber-neckers, I receive confirmation of one thing that I already know that I am not. As told to me and millions of others worldwide by Larry Birkhead when he stepped up to the podium, I am not the father of Anna Nicole's baby.

I'd like to think that he was directly addressing me when he shouted, "I told you so!" to the crowd. I'd like to believe that because when he said that he was looking in the direction of a sweating Texan that had just hollered "Give em hell Larry!" from the window of a taxi passing just a few yards away.

My driver isn't real chatty; in fact he hasn't spoken since we left the airport. When the traffic finally thins after leaving the courthouse block he glances in his rear view mirror and remarks, "I wish she'd a had dat beby in da states."

It's raining buckets when my alarm rings the next morning, and the Nassau airport is leaking buckets when I arrive there to catch my flight to Crooked Island. Miraculously, though, my flight leaves on time and arrives at Crooked International a few minutes ahead of schedule.

So far, so good. I've witnessed Larry's proud moment, I've had no flight delays, and my luggage pile has arrived intact. I'm now ready to relax, and fish, and photograph, with a week to mentally prepare for the impending travel debacle on the way home. And since that fiasco will take several pages to adequately flesh out, I've decided to briefly chronicle the six fishing days in a laundry list of succinct observation.

———

Crooked Island is near the bottom of the Bahamas and its proud three hundred, or so, inhabitants are a content and delightful assembly. Most of them are related, and if they're not, they still know what everyone else is up to.

Electricity came to Crooked just a few years ago, and when I asked one of the locals what they did before the window units were installed, he said they sweated a lot.

Crooked Island is made of limestone with a little sand sprinkled around the edges. If you need to build a fence, or a home, or a road you will build it from rock or rocklike byproducts. If you die there it will take a long damn time to dig a proper hole for your committal.

Some Bahamian guides wear the word "Bonefish" before their first name. I've asked several of them if there is a certain set of worldly angling criteria or level of guiding accolade that must be met before one can earn that title. Their responses indicated that it's a fuzzy and subjective matter, but each of them independently suggested that I'm not ready to be called "Bonefish Tosh."

Car horns in the U.S. are most often used to emphasize a scowl, a shaken fist, a Howard Dean scream, or an extended middle finger. Car horns on Crooked Island are used to accent a pleasant smile and a polite wave.

There are a few tarpon milling around Crooked Island and they're not very sophisticated. Mine ate a big tandem-hook cuda fly tied on a wire leader.

On Crooked Island there are tiny insects that can fly unimpeded through window screen mesh. Some people consider them only a mild annoyance, and some are allergic to their bites and they'll return home with a shotgun spray of reddish welts on their exposed surfaces. You'll learn which category you're in within 5-10 minutes of your arrival.

Dogs on Crooked Island do not have papers and they're typically fairly agile because sand crabs and lizards are a big part of their diet.

———

On the morning of April 18th my Bahamasair flight to Nassau is to depart Crooked Island at 10:05 a.m. Based upon their reputation, it seems ambitious that they would devise their schedules in five-minute increments. They'd receive considerably fewer hate letters if they would quote "between daybreak and lunch," or perhaps, "sometime on Wednesday" as their intended departure time.

But the plane is sitting proudly on the tarmac when we arrive at the airport at 9:00 a.m., and by 9:20 there's a bustle of activity around the fuselage that might indicate a timely departure. I'm pleasantly surprised when the gatekeeper calls us to board at 9:40 and I'm positively loopy when the cabin door closes and the props begin to whir at precisely 10:02. Is it possible that I'll have a flawless trip home?

As the rumbling turboprop taxis away from the terminal, I'm looking out the window with a nice view of the impending Bahamasair goatfuck that I thought I was about to avoid. When our "pilot" swings wide left as he's turning onto the runway, the left rear wheel of the airplane rolls over one of the runway lights. There is nothing delicate about the result. The tire explodes and the light is ground into the gravel like a toadstool stomped by a fat kid. To those that didn't witness the incident, I suppose the resulting rapid loss of tire pressure must have sounded a like a small bomb blast. The lady sitting across the aisle is screaming and her husband looks like he might have just shifted some luggage into his Ex Officios.

As the plane rolls to a halt, all terrorist rumors in the cabin are quickly squelched by numerous passengers, besides me, that had witnessed the blowout. Magazines and barf bags are now being used as fans as the cabin heats up and the pilots descend the staircase and convene under the shade of the portside wing. One of them kicks at the tire and the other jabs at the crumpled light stanchion and blue glass fragments with the toe of his loafer. When they look up at the row of windows full of pissed-off faces, they tandemly turn their backs and begin to mutter and gesticulate and harmonize their defense.

"Lady and gentlemens," the attendant chirps over the PA after the pilots have re-boarded, "it seems that we'll have a slight delay this morning due to an issue of mechanical nature."

A collective groan rises among the stranded.

"We will need each of you to deplane for a time while we address the problem."

I glance at my watch at 10:16 a.m. I had purposely scheduled a four-hour layover between my Crooked/Nassau flight and my Nassau/Austin connection on American. Was I smart, or was I not smart enough?

The fellow ahead of me in the aisleway turns to his wife as we shuffle through the stagnant cabin toward the aft doorway.

"Surely, this won't take long," he announces with buoyancy.

Surely you've never flown Bahamasair.

I suppose that the single cinder block building that comprises Crooked International would be more than sufficient for passengers quickly passing through. They probably wouldn't notice the lack of seating, dining, air conditioning, and functioning toilets.

My first stop, having a hunch that we might be there awhile, is the pair of vending machines on the sidewalk in front of the terminal. The drink selection is easy: eight quarters buys me two bottles of water. The snack decision is a bit more complex. I quickly rule out all of the slouching, melted chocolate bars that will never properly spin out of their curly wire holders. I also pass on the bags of salt, oil, and chip-like items that will force me to scrounge more quarters for more water. The Famous Amos cookies seem like a safe bet; four more quarters buys me a bag of chocolate chips.

My next stop is a piece of shade under a squat coconut palm where I take a seat in the sand and fish my phone from my backpack. American Airlines assures me that there are plenty of seat options from Nassau back to Austin, as long as I can depart Crooked Island by 2:30 p.m.

Four hours. Surely they can change a tire in four hours?

As the first hour of our fiasco ticks away, the following events transpire: a group of passengers gets conned into a game of dominoes with a group of locals. The remaining six bottles of water are purchased from the vending machine. A small fortune is lost on melted chocolate selections. The toilets fill up and become inoperable. It gets significantly hotter. The tire is not fixed.

At 11:30 a.m. I leave my sandy spot and walk into the terminal for a status check. The surly, yet indifferent, Bahamasair agent explains that another plane is being sent down from Nassau because Crooked International has no spare tire for our plane.

"When did that plane leave Nassau?" I ask.

"An hour from now," she replies.

I glance at my watch, again, and cipher the potential schedule aloud, "12:30 departure; a one hour flight; thirty minutes to board; another hour flight. That puts us in Nassau at 3:00, right?"

"Do *what*?"

At 1:00 the rescue plane hasn't landed, but an enterprising local that owns the best restaurant on the island has arrived with box lunches for everyone. Tuna salad on home baked bread, potato salad, a pickle spear, oatmeal cookies, and a bottle of water. I thank her profusely and ask her how much for the lunch. "No worries, honey," she beams, "the airline is taking care of it."

It occurs to me that she's done this before. I bet she begins each Bahamasair arrival day by making ninety box lunches, and I hope she's soaking those jackasses for $50 per meal.

At 1:50 p.m. a propeller drone rises over the mangroves and a small turboprop skids into view and buzzes up to the terminal building. I don't pay it much mind until someone standing nearby exclaims, "Good gosh, will you look at that!" Two persons wearing Bahamasair maintenance attire climb from the Cessna and roll a gigantic tire out of the back seat. A huge hydraulic jack is unloaded next. They have sent down a plane, just as promised.

At 2:30 p.m. our wounded blue and yellow albatross has been jacked up, and one of the pilots is straining with a giant lug wrench while the maintenance crew stands in the shade and watches. The domino game has broken up and a trail has been blazed through the mangroves to an alternate restroom site.

I again dial American Airlines to explore my options. "Well there's no chance that you'll get into Austin tonight," the agent explains as she pecks away at her keyboard. "I can get you into Fort Lauderdale tonight on a flight that leaves Nassau at 7:30, and then you can depart for Austin at 6:20 tomorrow morning."

I look at my watch again. *That's five hours from now... surely...*

At exactly 4:07 p.m., the jack is rolled away and a smattering of sarcastic applause erupts from the passengers that are standing and sitting and sweating in small gatherings around the premises.

Once we're seated inside the 114-degree cabin, the attendant is about to start her safety spiel when a feverish middle-aged lady on the brink of homicide hollers out, "We heard that CRAP nine hours ago, can we get this PLANE in the air, already?"

Seventy minutes later we land in Nassau. Three hours after that American Airlines deposits me in Fort Lauderdale. At 9:40 the next morning I arrive home in Austin, exactly nineteen hours past due.

A number of weeks pass before I get a written response from Bahamasair. According to their investigation of my complaint, there was no pilot error that caused my travel delay on April 18, 2007. Both pilots agreed that the flat tire was caused by normal wear. They refuted my accusation that a joyride through the grass and a smushed runway light had anything to do with it. They concluded by explaining that they would not be reimbursing me for my motel room in Fort Lauderdale, a small pizza, a quart of beer, cab fare, and my $11 pay-per-view purchase of *Borat*, because they are not responsible for delays caused by weather or normal wear on their airplanes.

I wonder if Larry and Anna Nicole would have gotten better treatment?

The Captain's New Clothes

In a nation of islands in a faraway tropical ocean there is a uterine-shaped atoll with great hordes of fast-running silver fish that prowl and forage across expansive temperate shallows. The atoll was first discovered by a British Captain who arrived there on the morning of a religious holiday, and so it was named.

After a number of years the peoples of the atoll recognized the need for an accommodation to house additional explorers, surfers, and other people of insolvency that would inevitably arrive. And so the government of the peoples built a hotel and named it after the Captain.

After more years an angler arrived and waded among the great hordes of silver fish and caught many and declared it "world class." Subsequently there arrived a selection of writers and facilitators and they officially documented the fishery as

133

"world class" and within months the shallows were being fished on a rotational basis by legions of anglers wearing quick-drying colors of mango, aqua, and coral and guided by the peoples of the atoll that were decreed professional. And because the Captain's was the only accommodation on the atoll, the writers and facilitators concurred that it was basic and quaint and charming. And so it became known.

For thirty years the atoll provided the legions with "world class" angling and the peoples prospered and soon they too wore colorful quick-drying shirts.

Eventually, however, an angler arrived and caught many of the silver fish, but he impudently suggested that the Captain's accommodation was perhaps *less* than basic, and not at all quaint or charming.

He suggested that the peoples had allowed the accommodation to decline. He wished that the towel bar in his room would actually hold one and he wished that he didn't feel the need to wear his wading boots in the shower. He asked for a breakfast cereal that wasn't Honey Bunches of Weevils but the peoples only shrugged. He understood that fresh lettuce was very expensive to import but he wondered why they didn't scratch lettuce from the menu altogether instead of serving the brownish and moldy root. He wondered why there was a large bloodstain on the tank lid of his toilet and he wished that he could sleep on a mattress that didn't have the topography of an empanada. At night there was a rhythmic and soothing surf outside his window, but his window was plugged by a clattering A/C unit that only marginally tempered the heat and the incessant yowling and screeching of feral cats screwing under the palms.

As word spread among the legions of the angler's distaste, most were relieved that someone had finally declared that the Captain's accommodation was less than basic. When word reached the peoples that a portion of the legion felt the Captain's accommodation was no longer quaint and charming and that it was actually crappy, a few of the peoples aspired to branch out and cash in on the dissention and so they built accommodations with functional towel bars and no bloodstains.

Soon, however, more anglers that didn't mind cat sex arrived at the Captain's accommodation to fill the void left behind by anglers seeking comfort, thereby increasing the total number of anglers. And since the great hordes of silver fish had not increased in number, they were now hooked more frequently and soon they became smarter. As the fish became smarter and the anglers caught fewer it was suggested to the peoples that the fishery might be in decline.

But the peoples only shrugged, because that's what their government had trained them to do.

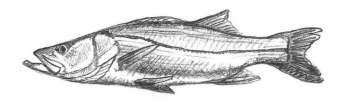

Pressed Ham

There was an immensely unpopular kid in my seventh grade class that we called The Turd. He was oversized with greasy hair and a sloping forehead and spit would form in the corners of his mouth when he talked. He was sullen and pugnacious with a vacuous stare. He wasn't a bully, and no one was afraid of him. He was just a punk and a master at stirring up trouble and then squirming out of it when teachers or parents showed up. He was never invited to parties, but he was always there; sulking in the shadows, lobbing water balloons, groping the girls, and spooning cheese dip into the tape player.

He was a real pillar of virtue.

For me, The Turd had never been more than an occasional annoyance, but at lunch on the last day of school, my girlfriend, in tears, showed me a suggestive note that The Turd had handed her after gym class. At that point the line had been drawn in the sand and I spent the rest of that day planning the ultimate beatdown on the scourge of our school.

When the bell rang, I bee-lined it for the curb and hid behind his bus. My plan was to board right behind him and hold the big slovenly goon captive until we reached his stop. At that point we'd disembark and I'd drop the hammer on him, away from school property, and hopefully right in front of his mom.

It was a grand plan, but the bus eventually pulled away from the school with nary a Turd on board. Walking back home, brooding and fuming, I reached the stop sign near my house just as a different bus from my school lurched alongside. When the bus pulled away, I looked up and saw The Turd's white, pimply ass pressed up against the back window. One of his little minions had told him about my stakeout, so The Turd invited himself over to that kid's house for the afternoon.

———

Join me, now, in the spring of 2008, where I'm staked out on the bow of a skiff near Chokoloskee, Florida. Cruising across a low-tide mud flat is an oversized, pugnacious punk with a sloping forehead and a vacuous stare.

Over the past fifteen years this fish has been nothing more than an occasional annoyance. In Belize, I found him lurking in the shadows under a mangrove where he refused a dozen presentations before I finally half-hitched my fly to the branch he was hiding under. In Costa Rica I made a thousand blind casts into the surf without a strike, and then a kid with a yo-yo and a live mullet walked up and caught him on his third toss. Near Marco Island, I found him crossing a sand flat and actually got a cast off without spooking him. He turned and followed the fly and then sucked it in coming straight at me. I flinched and pulled it right out of his mouth. On that same trip, while blind casting at high tide, he rose from the depths and blasted my streamer. For about three seconds I thought I had a chance when he ran for open water. Three seconds later he was back in the mangroves and I was stripping in a shredded leader. In the Yucatan I conceded the bow to Tom Bie while I shot photos and he caught a 40-incher on his first cast.

Big snook are a pain in the ass. I've caught plenty of the little minions, but I can't seem to drop the hammer on the big, slovenly goon.

And now, once again, I'm facing an opportunity to purge this irritation from my system. He's cruising along, pushing a bow wake, but a sandbar is blocking our approach and we can pole no closer.

By some miracle, I launch an impossibly long and tight loop and drop the fly about a foot from his nose. The explosion echoes across the lagoon, and when I strip and come tight I'm thinking that I've finally exorcised the demon. The Turd has nowhere to hide—not a snag in sight. There are no loops around my rod butt, and my leader is freshly tied. He thinks about running, and he thinks about jumping, but then he does neither.

He just sulks, and wallows, and shakes his head, and that's when the fly pops out.

As I stand there, brooding and fuming and wishing I could cry like a seventh-grade girl, the school bus pulls away with a white, pimply ass pressed against the back window.

Creature Comforts

How do you define the word remote?

No, I'm not talking about the little handheld clickers that perpetuate our sedentary lifestyles. I'm referring to the meaning of remote as it applies to travel and fishing.

I've often thought that a good litmus test of that word might involve the question of survival. How long could I make it in a particular far-flung locale if I was dropped off with nothing more than the clothes on my back?

That question came to mind when I caught my first aerial glimpse of Ragged Island through the windshield of a chartered twin-prop. The bustling Bahamian capitol of Nassau was 240 miles behind us. The Dominican Republic was 350 miles straight ahead. Seventy miles off our starboard wing was the port village of Gibara, Cuba. Between those waypoints was a seemingly endless expanse of open ocean.

When we buzzed and circled Duncan Town, Ragged's only settlement, my friend Ted Mendrek and I pressed our noses to the Plexiglas and began comparing observations.

"Not a very big island."

"Nope."

"Beautiful flats; looks like good wading."

"Yep."

"How many people live here?"

"No clue."

"Are those *goats* standing on the roof of that shack?"

A moment later our pilot lined us up with Ragged's hard-scrabble runway, which appeared sufficiently long even though it terminated at the edge of a huge turtle grass flat. Out of habit, I fished my phone from my backpack and switched it on as we rolled to a stop near a small shack at the end of the strip. After searching briefly for a signal, my electronic lifeline began buzzing and chiming and downloading emails.

Dammit.

Thirty minutes later, Ted and I were stringing up rods on the front stoop of Maxine's Guest House while the goats grazed about and the chickens pecked in the sand and the locals paraded past with smiles and waves and pleasant greetings.

There was a restaurant and cold beer on the island. Maxine's had running water, sheeted beds, and window units. There were undoubtedly bonefish, and hopefully the other species that prompted our collection of big rods, wire, and streamers.

We had already made contact with our host, Jason Owens, and soon we'd be meeting our guides.

It occurred to me, at that point, that we hadn't exactly reached the end of the earth, but I was pretty sure we could see it from where we were standing.

While researching for this trip, I learned that someone of authority once wrote a succinct history of Ragged Island and the rest of the world apparently took that person for his word. Every Google entry that I found about Ragged, and there aren't very many, listed the same verbatim facts:

Ragged Island is a small island (9 square miles) in the Southern Bahamas. Until recently it had an active salt industry, the salt ponds having been developed in the 19th Century by a Mr. Duncan Taylor, after whom Duncan Town, the only settlement, is named.

That's it. Apparently that's the entire written record of Ragged Island. If you want to learn more, you'll need to charter a flight or a boat. During our stay I asked several of the locals if there were any direct descendants of Duncan Taylor still living on the island. None of them could confirm any ancestral ties to "Mista Doon-kin" but they all held him in high regard.

This trip came about by way of Angling Destinations in Wyoming. Months earlier, they had divulged plans to build two new lodges in the Bahamas. They described the unexplored fishery on Ragged Island and explained their need for guinea pigs and photos. Their new lodge was still a few weeks shy of completion when we arrived, but Maxine's provided a comfortable alternative.

Ragged Island's umbilical cord is a weekly mail boat delivery from Nassau. You can therefore imagine the frustration when the mail boat might show up carrying 2x6's instead of 2x4's, or two-inch PVC instead of one-inch. At that point construction grinds to a halt and there's only one thing you can do until next Thursday's return shipment:

Go fishing.

Within two hours of our arrival, Ted and I were aboard a skiff with guide, Marvin, pushing us up a mangrove creek on the afternoon flood. The creek eventually fed into a big lagoon where we found a mob of schoolie bonefish and a host of larger pairs and singles that were milling and tailing over a soft, dark bottom.

As it turned out, that one inland lagoon was the only soft flat that we fished during our stay. The majority of Ragged's flats are hard sand, and some of them are so clean you can wade them barefoot. We found singles, pods, and enormous schools that varied from downright stupid during floodtide sessions, to characteristically fussy when they'd push onto the sand with the new water barely covering their backs.

One aspect of Ragged Island's fishery that we found especially intriguing was the pristine and intense predator/prey relationship. There were barracudas on every flat, some of them gargantuan, and they were not shy about hammering a fly, a tube lure, or a hooked bonefish. Leave your ankle bracelets at home, and if you have a fish tattoo on your calf, you might want to bring a tube sock to cover it up.

The cudas were a nuisance, in some places, but there were plenty of sharks around to keep them honest. On the flats they were mostly lemons in the two-three foot range; they were always trolling, always looking. We only lost a couple of bonefish to sharks, but we had to think and react fast to avoid them.

Along the channel edges the game changed significantly. On our second afternoon we were admiring a swirling school of rooting bonefish when we saw a four-foot cuda lurking on the fringe of their mud plume. While rigging up a wire leader, we watched him repeatedly circle and then tear through the school. After a couple of close sniffs at a streamer fly we decided to toss him the meat-n-taters rig. When the cuda hit the tube lure he launched himself from the water in a spectacular greyhounding display. After shooting some photos and releasing the fish, we were about to pole out of the area and check another spot when we heard a tremendous commotion on the edge of the flat.

The tired barracuda had swum over near a deep mangrove creek where he bumped into the resident alpha predator. The big bull shark caught the cuda just behind the dorsal and cut it in half with a single bite. After poling over and inspecting the part that the shark didn't eat, Captain Marvin, shook his head and flashed a grin.

"Dis a pretty tuff neybahood."

Later that afternoon we lost our sunlight to a line of thunderstorms, so Marvin took us over to a blue hole to show us a bit more of Ragged Island's voracious food chain. After anchoring on the upcurrent side of the hole, Marvin handed me a dive mask and suggested that I a take peek below. Leaning over the gunnel, I dipped the faceplate in the water and observed an extraordinary display of life and death swimming in a slow and methodical circle. At varying depths there were sharks and cudas patrolling among schools of ladyfish, jacks, and snappers. On the floor of the hole, about thirty feet down, was a school of circling bonefish. Everyone appeared happy and well-behaved, but that quickly changed when Ted dropped a Clouser into the hole and a bar jack made the mistake of eating it.

For the next two hours, we used up several yards of wire leader, ruined a lot of flies, and laughed ourselves silly as the once placid blue hole turned into a frothing and bloody cage fight.

The first jacks that we hauled in were sacrificed for chum, which we used to bring the entire melee to the surface for sight casting. Turns out that the only smart ones in the bunch were the bonefish. They knew where they could remain safe, and they stuck to the bottom of the hole like carpet tiles. On occasion, if a Clouser made it to the bottom without getting eaten, one of the bones would pick it up and then our challenge was to fight it to the surface before a shark could catch it. None of the bonefish were eaten, but we had a near miss when a two-pounder was hoisted from the surface with a snapping and lunging lemon shark right on its tail. Incidentally, we learned that bonefish can swim just as fast vertically as they can laterally. Each one that we released back into the hole would dive for the bottom like a slimy torpedo.

On the morning of our third day, we were poling a bonefish flat on the southwest side of the island when the outline of a sailing-type vessel appeared on the horizon. As the boat approached, we could make out dozens of people packed onto the sagging decks of a forty-foot wooden sloop with a tattered, vinyl mainsail that was fashioned from a Volkswagen dealership banner.

"What's up with that?" Ted asked Marvin as the sailboat dropped anchor inside the reef.

"Hea-shuns," he said, "You gonna see some shit go down, nah."

When we returned from fishing that afternoon, the troupe of Haitian refugees had been led up the hill and sequestered in the front yard of the Ragged Island Police Station. Immigration had already arrived from Exuma, and Marvin explained that the uninvited migrants would be escorted from the island at dawn.

"We don't put up wif dat," Marvin explained. "Dey come hea'ya and dey steal our boats in da night."

We were told that they were trying to reach Nassau but veered off course. Oddly, they in no way resembled a group of refugees from a leaking overcrowded boat that had been at sea for six days. Many of the ladies were in dresses and heels. They looked like they'd been to the mall, or maybe a church social.

Early the next morning, the group was lined up and counted before they were marched down to the dock where their transport vessel awaited. There were 120 Haitians that started the march, but only 116 reached the boat landing. After a half-day panicked lockdown of the island, the four escapees were found hiding in a mangrove thicket north of town. We didn't see them when they were finally nabbed and brought to the dock, but we were told that they weren't walking on their own.

By the time we finished our last day of fishing, the Haitian 120 had departed and Ragged Island had returned to its traditional placid and peaceful existence. Doors and windows were unlocked, laundry was flapping in the breeze, and the feral dog population had resumed chasing feral poultry. Plans were underway to fireball the refugee ship and set it adrift, and the residents of Duncan Town were smiling and waving, again.

The next morning we boarded our charter flight home with sunburns, lineburns, and a fresh dose of perspective. While Ragged Island isn't completely immune to the passage of time and the encroachment of progress, it doesn't fit the mega-resort development profile and the bonefish flats won't abide more than a few anglers per week—nor will the locals.

If you're looking for an authentic out-island experience, then Ragged Island is unquestionably worth the challenges of getting there. Just don't show up unannounced.

Blow The Man Down

Wikipedia states that wind is a function of pressure gradients and the forces of Coriolis, buoyancy, and friction. There are geostrophic winds, ageostrophic winds, and thermal winds. Their editors explain those terms in tedious detail if you're interested in learning more.

With respect to fishing: slick calm days are good for spotting redfish tails and rolling tarpon at a considerable distance. And because those are quasi-unintelligent species you can still get close on a glassy, sweaty day without goading the spook reflex that resides in their smallish brains. Placid and still is also good for sailfish, dorado, tuna and other species that swim in deep water because you can reach them and catch them without risk of spinal compression or refunding your breakfast.

A moderate breeze is good for bonefish, permit, and

over-fished trout streams where a little surface ripple can disguise an unstealthy approach, a bad cast, or an ugly fly. A little wind is also good for bass, carp, and panfish, because it blows mulberries and baby birds and Cheetos from the bank into the water.

A sustained wind that peels back your eyelids and impedes close-range conversation is pretty much bad for everything except sea trout in Tierra del Fuego and whatever you might fish for in the Bering Sea. In those places the wind doesn't bother the fish; the burden of acclimation falls upon us hominids.

There are lots of expressions and labels that are used to describe the wind. It can howl and scream and moan and wail. It can ripple and wisp and breeze and puff. It can hammer and gust and pound and blast. When it wraps around high pressure, it blows from the north. When it's pulled in by low pressure, it sucks from the south.

Culture and geography also shape the depiction of wind. The yanks laud their Nor'easters and the westerners have their Chinooks and Santa Annas. In the heartland there are Alberta Clippers and the ubiquitous Shit Winds that envelop those living downwind from cattle feed lots. Lucky mariners who rode out hurricanes in the days before televised weather sensationalism had their own pet name for the wind; they called it The Devil's Voice.

Is there an angling sect that's immune to the variables of wind? Well, the gear manufacturers seem to have their bases covered. For calm days they sell us one-weights, silky tippets, miniscule flies, vented clothing, and big hats. For blustery days they pimp their rocket tapers, cone heads, bombproof outerwear, and fast-action rods that can punch a parakeet into the teeth of a gale.

Ultimately, I suppose, the wind can best be defined in terms of cause and effect. To fully understand its influence on fly fishing, one should consider the popular claims and excuses that go along with it.

Perspective	Statement	Translation
Angler	It's too windy to fly fish	I'm deadly with a spinning rod
Angler	I've got a wind knot	I've got a casting knot
Angler	So, when is the best time to fish here?	I prefer light and variable winds. Are any of those days available next spring?
Guide	The wind is your friend	Deal with it dude. I'm not giving up a payday because of a ten-knot breeze
Guide	Tighten up that loop and you'll get more distance	Your cast looks like a bad marriage of the hammer throw and Chinese ribbon dancing
Guide	Let's clip off that dropper and fish a single nymph	I'd rather dig one hook from my scalp than two
Forecaster	Continued sunny and breezy through Monday	Call the airline or find a bar

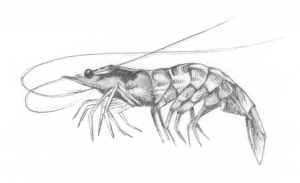

Hath Hell Frozen?

I hadn't planned to be in New Orleans when the Saints played in their first Super Bowl; it just worked out that way. They were 6-0 back in October when I booked my redfish dates with Bryan Carter. At that time everyone in Louisiana knew they'd still be playing on February 7th, 2010, but most folks outside the Bayou State hadn't caught on.

On Saturday, before the game, I bumped into the first Saints fans when I was boarding my flight from Austin to New Orleans. They were middle-aged white folk sporting fleur de lis cheek tattoos and Reggie Bush jerseys and shouting "WHO DAT?" at anyone who dared make eye contact.

When I arrived in New Orleans the excitement was palpable. Between my gate and the rent car shuttle I counted eleven Reggies and sixteen Drews. "I've been there for this team since day one," said one bulging man with a red nose and a rope of black and gold beads around his neck. "I lived through the Aints years. I wore the damn bag on my head!"

On the way to Port Sulphur we picked our way through parades and traffic jams and streetside revelry. Car flags flapped, horns honked, and meats flamed on grills. It was thirty hours before the kickoff of a game being played 668 miles away.

The next morning, Bryan picked us up at Woodland Plantation. It was never mentioned, but it was understood that we'd be off the water in time for pregame. While poling the flats and slinging hair at large and reddish "marsh donkeys," Bryan recounted his early years as a Saints fan. "I'm not sure how old I was when my dad took me to my first game, but I do remember that the Redskins beat their asses like 48-3. I didn't know much about football back then, but after that game I had a pretty good idea that the Saints really sucked."

By gametime a small crowd of anglers and locals had gathered at the bar back at Woodland. At first it felt odd swilling scotch in their Spirits Hall, a converted church (circa 1883), but owner Foster Creppel explained that since it was once a Catholic facility, we would all be assured of our spots in the hereafter. Foster and his crew were decked out in their fan gear and he nervously admitted just before kickoff, "I've been waiting forty-three years for this, but I guess all I'm really hoping is they don't beat us too bad."

For the next three hours we dined on oysters, fried shrimp, boudin, gumbo, and red snapper while screaming ourselves silly over every Drew Brees completion. By the fourth quarter, the

Colts were folding and the Who Dat Nation was clinging to a tenuous victory. When Terry Porter pick-sixed Peyton Manning at the 3:23 mark, the Woodland faithful erupted in a deafening cacophony of screams, high-fives, barking, flying chest-bumps, and spilled drinks. I can't even imagine the chaos on Bourbon Street at that particular moment.

There was brief discussion of a road trip into the French Quarter, but one of Foster's staff had heard that all roads leading into the city had been jammed since noon. The forecast was calling for clear and still the next morning, and we weren't willing to miss a rare perfect winter day on the flats.

While Katrina defined the resiliency of New Orleans and its people, in my mind there's still an underlying feeling of pessimism when viewing the city from an airplane window. It's a low-lying place that is blatantly susceptible to natural forces that can spawn social chaos and economic collapse.

For now, though, all is good in the Big Easy. The tourists are back, the fish are tailing, the marsh is still intact, and the loveable losers of the NFL have exorcised their demons. Live it up New Orleans, and let's hope that the winds, tides, and free agency keep you in a good light.

Note: two months after I wrote this, British Petroleum soused Louisiana with a miserable calamity known as the "Deepwater Horizon Spill." It cost BP around 20 billion in cleanup and fines, but it may be decades before we know if that was enough.

Seven Days With Alex

June 28, 2010 - 11:30 a.m.

I've had a bad Internet connection for the past couple of days so I haven't paid much attention to the weather. This morning, there were eight inches of new water on the flats that have just produced the best stretch of redfishing I've ever had. It's been glass calm for six days with wagging schools, waking singles, line-burned fingers, and shredded thumbs. Heaven on a six-weight. Now I'm online and staring at the spinning, building cloud mass that has somehow completely flooded our redfish flats from 800 miles distant. His/her name is Alex.

June 29, 2010 - 9:00 p.m.

My wife and kids arrived and we're planning to stick it out through the Fourth of July weekend. Alex is now a tropical storm and chugging northwestward across the Bay of Campeche. The Weather Channel sensationalists are predicting a late Wednesday landfall near the mouth of the Rio Grande. I tried to fish this morning but the tides were up another foot. It takes a really tall redfish to tail in waist-deep water. When I got back to the dock the water was lapping at the boards. My boat is now on the trailer and we're preparing for the big hunker.

June 30, 2010 - 10:00 a.m.

Alex is now a hurricane and the dock is underwater. The wind is sustained from the East at thirty and the buoy readings off Port Aransas are showing incoming swells at seventeen feet. We've braved the crowds of grimy clamoring locals at the grocery and Blue Marlin Video Rental. Redfish are no longer on the radar.

June 30, 2010 - 5:30 p.m.

We watched Jim Cantore for as long as we could stand him, then we drove out to the beach to prove (to ourselves) that we're tougher than he is. We are now about 250 miles north of the projected landfall. On the Horace Caldwell pier, we staggered into winds gusting to sixty to watch the surfers jump from the T-head and ride the massive swells back to the beach. These guys don't get many epic surf days on the Texas Coast, so they take advantage of the ones they get. They're beat down, board-chafed, and glassy-eyed. They've been out here for hours. A squall line moves in and blasts us with needle rain. Jim Cantore is a wimp.

July 1, 2010 - 4:00 p.m.

Alex is now eighty miles inland near San Fernando, Mexico, still a hurricane but weakening. The water is still over the dock and the wind is still cranking. The backside rain bands are blasting us in two-hour intervals. We've played countless hands of cards and all of our board games. The kids beat the wife and me in Pictionary because I couldn't draw a recognizable picture of a yam. I enjoyed *Crazy Heart*, but to me Jeff Bridges now seems oddly out of character if he's not wearing jelly sandals and drinking Caucasians in a bowling alley.

July 2, 2010 - 3:00 p.m.

The winds are down to about twenty but the water is still up. We're now in a middle moon phase with weak tides. That's not good. We need a gigantic toilet flush to get us back into redfish. We tried beach lounging but it was knee-deep in storm flotsam and stinking piles of Sargasso weed. This is Port A's biggest weekend of the year and the island is deserted. There's no wait for a table at any of the restaurants that are open. I'm sure that M. Knight Shyamalan is good at something, but making great movies ain't it.

July 3, 2010 - 7:00 p.m.

The sun is out and the boat is back in the water. We lost about a foot of tide, today, so my son and I went for a little recon paddle in our kayaks. We saw lots of tall, windswept water and no redfish. The island is starting to fill with tourists, but since the beach is a mess, they're stacked into the swimming pools like whales in gymnasiums. Screaming kids, back hair, exposed cracks, and sun-fried arm dangles. To the tattooed size-sixteen basting in the hot tub with a Natty Light and a cigarette: were there no mirrors in the dressing room when you bought that bikini?

July 4, 2010 - 10:15 p.m.

I must have hit the refresh button on the online tide chart a thousand times today. It's dropping slowly, but we still need to lose another foot of water before fishing is even remotely viable. We spent the day with friends and stuffed ourselves with fajitas, trimmings, and margaritas. The evening firework display was nice, but next year I'm loading some patriotic tunes on my iPod so I don't have to listen to drunken redneck whoops after each rocket's red glare. Tomorrow is our last shot for fishing; I have to be back in Austin on Tuesday.

July 5, 2010 - 8:00 a.m.

My summer 2010 redfish window has now closed. The tide was back up to the dock boards this morning and the wind was cranking southeast at twenty. As a diversion, we winched the kids out of bed to watch the baby sea turtle liberation. These are the endangered Kemp's Ridleys that nest each summer on North Padre Island. For maximum yield, all of the nests are sequestered and hatched in the lab. The babies are then released into the surf at sunrise while volunteers distract the seagulls with bags of Fritos. At daybreak we reached the entrance to the National Seashore and found a fire truck blocking the way. The beach road was closed because some genius felt the need to celebrate our country's independence by firing a Roman candle into the dunes and torching the entire island. When we returned to Port Aransas our air conditioner was on the fritz. At this point I haven't gotten an official diagnosis from the repairman, but for now I'm blaming that bastard, Alex.

Cock of the Rock

It wasn't the first roosterfish I caught that turned me all sappy and prophetic. That one came on our first day in Baja when we were teasing them up to a panga with live sardines. The one of which I was most proud was the rooster that I caught from the beach. No chum, no outboards, bare feet on blistering sand, running, sweating, huffing, and flogging.

It was our last day, and to that point I'd screwed up on beach roosters every way possible. Most notable was the 40-pounder that combed up on my fly and was actually opening its mouth to eat when I started back peddling to move the fly faster and fell on my ass in the sand.

Gone.

"It happens," said Jeff DeBrown, our guide. "Last week a client missed a grande when he tripped over a log."

Roosters don't eat things that stop.

With the sun dropping and the light fading, I finally connected on a special needs beach rooster that was obviously unaware that a movie had been made about him. He was well south of 40 pounds, but he was MY rooster, caught the hard way, and I was damn proud to have him. After the photos and the release, I turned to Jeff and my buddy Mike Siegman with a big cheesy grin and said, "I could die tomorrow."

Twelve hours later, at 5:00 a.m., I awoke with what I first thought was a major bout of the tourista. While laying there sweating and cramping and pondering a sprint to the toilet, I replayed last night's dinner. Only a couple of beers…no tequila… the grilled dorado?

I rolled over and tried to get comfortable.

Didn't help.

I went to the toilet and sat.

Nothing.

I crawled back in bed.

By 5:30 the pain had moved to my lower back on the right side. I woke up Mike and said, "Hey man, something's bad wrong, here."

I was soaked in sweat and having trouble breathing. It felt like someone was grinding the heel of their boot into my back. After writhing around and trying to get comfortable, I finally stood up to try and get some relief. When I hit vertical, a wave of nausea came over me and I sprayed last night's catch of the day across the room.

Mike jumped out of bed, "Dude, you need help."

A bit later he returned with Jeff and John, the owner of Rancho Leonero. Jeff was carrying a Ziploc full of Pepto Bismol, Imodium, and such. He took one look at me and said, "These won't help."

John asked, "Where's the pain?"

I couldn't answer so I motioned toward my lower back.

Five minutes later I was in the front seat of Jeff's truck being sped over washboard roads toward the Ameri-Med clinic in Los Barriles. The attending doctor was a friend of John's and he had already been called. The clinic wasn't officially open when we arrived, but we were greeted by a pleasant nurse who told us that the doctor was on his way.

A bit later he walked into the room. Smiling, polite, perfect English. After looking me over and asking a few questions he said, "Three possibilities Mr. Brown."

He first poked around on my lower abdomen, "Any pain there?"

I shook my head.

"That rules out appendicitis." He prodded a different spot, "How about here, the pancreas?"

"No."

He then rolled me over on my stomach and pressed with his thumb on a spot on my back that was obviously marked "HURL." When I blasted what was left in my stomach across the clinic, the nice doctor said, "Mr. Brown, you have a kidney stone."

I looked at Mike, he looked at Jeff, we all looked at the doctor.

"Unfortunately, there's nothing I can do for you here," he

explained. "You need to be in the hospital in San Jose del Cabo, and if I've misdiagnosed then it could cause problems if I treat you here."

An ambulance was called and an IV bag of saline solution was hung above my gurney. "It's seventy miles, Mr. Brown. We'll get you there quickly and safely."

At that point I replayed the numerous van trips I'd made between San Jose del Cabo and The East Cape. No shoulders, hairpin turns, potholes, wayward livestock, decrepit bridges, lawless drivers.

Paving new ground here, folks...

Mike hopped into the front seat while they clanked me into the back. Jeff returned to the hotel to pack up our things in case, by some miracle, we could still make our flights home later that day.

Once on the road, the pain started building in waves. Every ripple on the asphalt sent a sucker punch into my trunk, and I could tell that the young attendant sitting with me in the back was wishing he'd gotten a different assignment that day.

Latin Americans are a somewhat pliable and affiliated lot. They believe wholly in their deity and they harbor a healthy fear of the godless. Maybe it was my fishbelly death pallor that spooked him, or maybe it was the smell of bile, and my writhing and cursing and clenched teeth. He wanted nothing to do with me. He was nervous and his hands were shaking as he swapped out my IV bag. He was squirmy and jukey and at one point I opened my eyes and caught him crossing himself.

I slept for some of the ride. It didn't seem like seventy

miles. The driver did a great job, and it was the siren that woke me when we hit the rush hour traffic going into San Jose. In hindsight, Mike said he probably shouldn't have answered the cell phone call from my wife while the siren was wailing, but he did enjoy flipping the switch to shoo the locals out of the road.

A few blocks from the hospital, we took a speed bump a little too fast, which again triggered my hurl reflex. The attendant saw it coming and scooted a bucket toward me with his foot. It was made of galvanized tin with a montage of Señor Frogs and Corona logos emblazoned across it.

By the time they wheeled me inside, the pain was indescribable. I couldn't speak, I couldn't move and my breaths were coming in rattled gasps. I thought back to what I said on the beach after releasing the rooster. I stared up at the shimmering halo around the fluorescent lights and considered a deific bargain to give up fishing altogether, but decided to wait first on the official diagnosis.

It was another Ameri-Med hospital, clean and well-staffed with modern equipment. A doctor was waiting and they wheeled me straight into x-ray. Within minutes they confirmed what the clinic in Los Barriles predicted.

Yep, it's a kidney stone.

They replaced the saline with a bag of Valium and Mike got back on the phone with my wife. What happened next renewed my faith in modern medicine and those who manufacture and administer it.

While the Valium dripped and the doctor explained the process of surviving a piece of jagged detritus lodged in a small delicate place, his words and the image of his face slowly transformed from a scratchy, garbled haze into startling clarity. I stopped sweating. The urge to puke went away. My jaw unclenched. My toes uncurled. My heart rate slowed, and my breathing returned to normal.

I looked up at the bag. It was still mostly full.

The doctor asked, "Feeling better, Mr. Brown?"

"…Ungh-huh…"

"We'll need to get your insurance squared away. Who's your carrier?"

"…Ummm…Blue Cross?"

"Ahhhh," he winced and changed the subject. "You should get to the airport and try to get home. Contact your doctor as soon as you arrive. It's going to get bad again when the medicine wears off, but I've given you enough for several hours of comfort. Drink lots of water, all you can handle."

Fifteen minutes later, we were paid in full—the whopping sum of $83—and I walked out of the hospital frisky as a pup. Two hours after that we checked in for our flights. At 7:30 p.m. I pulled into my driveway in Austin and hugged my wife and kids. I told them the entire story, drank a glass of water, and went to bed.

The pain returned at midnight. By the time I got to my doctor the next morning I had developed a nasty kidney infection. By the next day I was back in the hospital, dehydrated, fevered, writhing in pain again, and twelve pounds heavier. I felt like a walking septic tank with a clogged pump.

The devil rock finally passed two nights later.

I had a lot of time to think about Baja and roosters and healthcare during my four days of personal hell. My local doctor says dehydration from chasing The Man up and down the beach probably caused the stone to jar loose. He also warned that I'm now susceptible to more of them.

I'll go back to Baja, and next time I'll drink more water. And next time I'll have a little baggie in my shaving kit marked "kidney stone meds." And next time I won't step through my line when I'm running. And next time I'll keep my fly moving when the grande gets behind it.

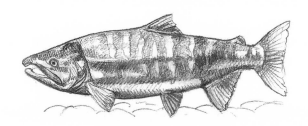

Dog Park

Reputations are a funny thing; easy to establish yet hard to shake. Once a bad rap is repeated often enough it becomes deeply impressed. Like soy sauce laundered into a white shirt.

From the Northwest, throughout Alaska, and around the Pacific Rim, there swims the denigrated bastard child among anadromous fish. Though quite the fighter on rod and line, the lowly chum salmon was labeled as poor food value many eons ago and therefore it gets much less love than its more palatable Pacific brethren.

The name "chum" has been traced back to the Chinook people, early tribal inhabitants of the Pacific Northwest. In their jargon *"tzum"* means, *spotted* or *marked*. A fitting tag given the chum's garish purple and red stripes that develop when they return from the ocean to their birth rivers.

Modern era Yup'ik and Inuit natives call them "dog salmon." This may refer to the vicious canines that sprout from the male's kype during spawning, yet some claim that the name comes from the native's preference of feeding chum salmon to their sled dogs.

More than their taste, I'm convinced that the chum salmon's real setback might be the timing of its spawning run. If they came in first, just after ice-out like king salmon typically do, there would be a lot more fanfare from anglers who have survived nine months of arctic winter swilling George Dickel and watching Jerry Springer re-runs. Conversely, if they arrived in late summer like coho salmon, one wouldn't care much about their taste when he's got freezers to fill and the clock is dropping 12 minutes of daylight per cycle.

Sadly, though, the chum arrives in mid-summer throughout most of Alaska, and since that's where most pay-to-fish anglers encounter him, his tainted standing has spread far and wide among the sporting legions.

Woe be the angler who has booked an expensive week in early July hoping to get in on the tail end of the Chinook run. There are still a few bright kings at tidewater, but most have turned red and pushed upriver for their spawn. The week is winding down, that fella still hasn't caught his king, and the chums are pouring into the river in droves. Cast, swing, chum, DANG! Cast, swing, chum, CRAP!

Then there's the meat-hauler who's targeting chrome sockeyes in mid-July. He's got his flossing rig deployed and an empty cooler ready to fill with glistening red slabs of omega protein. He casts into the horde, his bobber dips, he thinks of dill and wood smoke, he readies his bonking stick…fresh sockeye! Nope…fresh chum…

Or the trout fan who books a late July week. The kings are all but done and the chums are now in their full-on goblin attire; olive backs and striped flanks with teeth like the Grinch. They're spawning and aggressive and slashing at every fly that drifts past. His six-weight bends and his drag screams and he thinks he's got the rainbow of a lifetime. YES!…wait…damn-it-to-hell…another chum.

And pity the coho angler in August. He's found a raft of chasing and rolling silvers, just in from the Bering Sea. He ties on a Pollywog and wakes it across the pool. A dime-bright silver turns and lines up for the surface grab. Lurching downcurrent, though, is a spawned-out zombie with fins dropping off and globs of mold covering its eyes. With mouth agape, the dying chum staggers blindly into the fly line, pulls the Pollywog into its cheesy maw, and forces the angler to handline the cadaver to the bank where he fights back the urge to puke while removing the hook…

FUCKING CHUMS!

On a mid-summer photo shoot to Alaska in 2011, we were targeting Dolly Varden on the Togiak River that were stacking up below the spawning chums and slurping their eggs. The catching was so good that it got silly. Double, triple, and quadruple Dolly hookups were common among our group and after a few hours we were looking for a new challenge.

When a raft of still-fresh chums pushed through, the

six-weights were stowed and the guides scrambled to prepare us for battle. With heavy rods and gaudy streamers we laid into the chums with dipnets at the ready.

While I photographed a particularly striking hook-jawed male, our guide poetically professed, "I think chum is a poor name for such a magnificent fish. I mean, seriously, they attack flies, they rip drag, and they're really cool to look at. I prefer to call them 'Calico Salmon.' Like a snowflake, each one unique in its beauty and design."

Just then we heard a shout from down the gravel bar. Another fellow in our group was straining against the butt of a deeply bent rod. Thrashing in the shallows in front of him was a 15-pound male, still bright from the sea with stripes barely showing. As chums go, it was about as nice a fish as one could hope for. He grabbed the chum by the tail, hoisted it aloft, and shouted, "Look at the size of THIS ugly bastard!"

Reputations are a funny thing.

Note: In July of 2013 I visited the Kanektok River to shoot photos for Deneki Outdoors at their Alaska West camp. On arrival we were greeted with smoked salmon fillets for appetizers that were among the best I've ever tasted. Smoker boss Dan Brevelle confessed that they were chums and his secret was a copious slather of salt and brown sugar brine before putting them in the smoke. I immediately thought back to everything I'd read about chum salmon tasting poorly and the Alaska natives that perpetuated that notion. Perhaps their palates are more refined than I presumed? Maybe seal blubber isn't as bad as it sounds.

Maashkinoozhe

That's how he was tagged eons ago by the first Ojibwa native that tangled with him. Loosely translated, "maashkinoozhe" means "ugly pike." The French came along later and called him masquinongé which, for all we know, means "big-ass fish that we can't catch."

While the muskellunge doesn't have much of a following among sporting artists, I think the "ugly" label is still a bit unfair. After hundreds of casts with a 10-weight, a sinking line, and a fly the size of a tandem bratwurst, my first maashkinoozhe was one of the more beautiful things I'd seen in a great while.

Before Hayward native Brad Bohen started posting musky-on-fly photos on Facebook, the State of Wisconsin wasn't really mentioned much as a destination fly-fishery. They've always had good smallmouth and trout fishing in S'consin, but the real buzz didn't start until Brad peppered the internet with abundant proof that muskies are a legitimate fly target, even for those who are only slightly deranged.

On a Sunday in October, 2011, I flew up to fish and photograph with Brad and his newly formed Musky Country Outfitters. After landing in the Twin Cities I rented a car and typed "Hayward" into my GPS. Driving through the rolling countryside east of the Minnesota line, I was immediately taken in by the charm and beauty of rural Wisconsin. It was just after harvest and the finely manicured cornfields were crowded with whitetails and Canada geese. In dairy country the barns and fences were all neatly painted, and the trademark black and white Holsteins looked like they'd just come back from the groomers. No ribs showing, no dripping snot, and no butt scours.

Maybe our Texas cattle eat too much cactus?

In the town of Cumberland I pulled over for gas at a country store that Norman Rockwell had obviously once visited. Out front they were selling log sculptures of black bears carved with chainsaws. There was a pumpkin stand surrounded by gathered corn shocks with colorful dried squashes and gourds hanging about. Inside there were fresh baked goods and cracker barrels and racks of Genuine Wisconsin Cheddar Cheese. Near the checkout they were selling Aaron Rodgers jerseys alongside t-shirts that explained Green Bay's true feelings about Brett Favre's defection to the Vikings—who they happened to be playing at *that* very moment.

At the counter, a lady wearing official green and yellow was watching the game on a small TV and all progress in the checkout line had stopped because it was fourth-and-five and the Vikings were just out of field goal range. When Favre's pass was batted down at the 30, a small chorus of cheers erupted in the Rockwell-Mart.

"Now who dahsn't believe in bad care-mah?" the clerk asked her patrons.

I paid her for a tank of gas and my bottle of "diet pahp" and as I turned to leave she said, "Have a greet day, and go Peckers!"

In Hayward, I passed the giant fiberglass musky statue and turned east toward the Chequamegon National Forest and the unofficial boundary of The North Woods. Within a few miles the towering pine canopy closed in and the highway narrowed as it wound through unending lake and river drainages.

At Boulder Lodge I was greeted by the owners and shown to my cabin. "Brad and the guys will be in after dark. They'll head to the bar as soon as they get in, so come on over after you're settled and we'll fix you a burger."

Beat down and bleary-eyed, Brad strode in round 8:30 with his fellow guides Chris Willen and Lucky Porter. They'd had a good day: three muskies to the boat, one a slab in the low-forties. As we drank a few beers they talked about their season and how it typically all comes down to the last few weeks before ice-up.

"You might hook into a great fish during any week of the summer, but the big gals get really anxious this time of year," Brad explained, "You're here at the right time. It's supposed to stay cold all week and they've got to eat."

It was 30 degrees at daybreak and Brad suggested a café

177

breakfast before we hit the river. Among gossiping deer and grouse hunters in varied patterns of blaze orange, we shoved down great heaps of artery spackle, thinned with steaming black coffee. The total bill was about four bucks a head and I knew walking out that my late lunch waiting in Brad's cooler would also be my early dinner.

At 8:45 a.m. I made my first official musky cast. At 4:30 I made my last cast of that day, and even though I felt like I'd covered every dark and tannic nook of the Chippewa River, I was fishless when we reached the takeout. At about 3:00 I had a good one rise up and mouth the fly on my 743rd cast of the day, but my delirious deadpan hookset didn't close the deal.

"That's why you booked three days," Porter said. "You'll get one tomorrow if your shoulder still works in the morning."

Muskies are apex predators and they don't get big by eating small food. At breakfast the next morning, I washed down some Advil with my coffee as Brad explained the evolution of their musky flies. "The profile of the fly is important, but they've also got to move water and make noise," he explained. "We stack them up with bucktail and make 'em as bulky as possible on the front end with lots of hackle and wiggle in the back. They're hell to cast, but we didn't start consistently moving fish until we started chunking these big flies."

And "chunking" is an apt description. There's nothing artful about musky casting. If you've never tried a water-load with a fly rod, Google it and learn it before you go. You'll squeeze in a lot more casts per day if you're not trying to keep a pound of wet deer in the air from dawn until dusk.

Day two started with clouds and drizzle and temps in the high 30's. "This is a musky day," Brad said as he backed his drifter down the ramp.

In the first run we were working through a slot of roiling water next to a big rockpile when a good fish slashed at the fly and missed. A bit further down we caught a small pike. Then we moved another small musky that wouldn't commit. "Keep pounding it," Brad said, "and don't forget your figure-eights."

Muskies, as Brad explained have an oddball habit of tracking flies all the way back to the boat. If the fly quietly slips from the water the fish will typically lose interest and turn back to its lair. That's where the figure-eight comes in. Standard musky M.O. requires that the angler strip in all but a few feet of leader. He then jams the rod tip in the water and loudly swirls the fly in a figure-eight pattern just below the surface. If there's a fish lurking beneath the boat but not ready to bite, the figure-eight often goads them into attack.

"They love that," Brad said. "And if you slack off on your figure-eights you'll miss a lot of opportunities."

The drizzle finally stopped just before lunch and as we approached a tight bend in the Chippewa, Brad spoke up and interrupted the monotony of casting. "Okay, Tosh, down past this bend on the right there's a big deep back-eddy next to a steep rock face. You're only gonna get one shot 'cause the current will catch us and drag us out, but I want you to smack that fly against the rock face and then let it drop into the eddy."

He rowed us through the tailout up above and into the chute; when the eddy appeared on the right he told me to start my cast. When my fly slapped the rock face and dropped into the hole, Brad pulled hard on the oars and held us briefly in place. "Okay strip it back and do your figure—"

The musky grabbed the fly on the second strip, then ran back into the eddy and boiled on the surface. Brad had to do some fancy oar work to keep us from spinning, but the current finally caught us and led us down the chute with the musky in tow. In a patch of frog water below the eddy, Brad nosed us onto the gravel bar just as the musky dug in for the final round. The whole fight lasted maybe thirty seconds, and as Brad slid him into the net I realized that my right hand was still clamped to the exact spot on my line that I'd been holding when the fish bit. It was a tight-line tug-of-war and neither of us had given ground.

After the high-fives and the photos, Brad rowed down to the lunch spot and we pulled in for a break. As we unpacked the cooler Brad fessed up that he had a solid hunch about that eddy. "We've caught three muskies out of that hole this season. If you asked me to describe a textbook musky spot, that would be it."

I asked him if there were any other spots on the Chippewa where he'd be brave enough to make a called shot on a fish that's incredibly tough to catch on a fly.

After a pause for thought he said, "No, not on this river."

Even though I'd tried to budget the number of tosses I'd made, my casting arm finally gave out around 3:30. Our final tally for the day was five muskies moved, three bites, and two caught. If you factored in a couple of pike, one Kamikaze smallmouth, skeins of geese overhead, and a ruffed grouse that buzzed us near the takeout, we'd had what North Woods guides would call a banner day.

On our last day we were joined by my friend and artist/guide Bob White, who lives just a couple hours west of Hayward on the St. Croix River. While Bob and I started the day casting and figure-eighting with conviction, we eventually let down our guard as the sun climbed higher and the temperatures warmed. Brad was working on the lyrics to a musky-fishing song, and given our proximity to Lake Superior he chose Gordon Lightfoot as its basis.

The legend lives on from the Chippewa on down
of the big lake they call Gitche Gumee...

After lunch the temperatures warmed into the sixties and we approached a long glassy run where Brad perked up and gave us a new charge. "We moved a really big one in here two weeks ago. Let's fish this hard and see if she's still around."

Bob and I started casting again with commitment as Brad back-stroked and held us as long as possible over each likely hold. We both made probably 30 to 40 casts through the run and when we reached the tailout Brad said, "We're not giving up that easy, I'm gonna row us back up and we'll change flies."

And so goes the donkeywork of musky fishing. With new sizes and colors we slogged back to the top and started casting again. Loooong shots...all the way to the bank...strip it back...figure-eights...backcast...water-load...do it again...

Does anyone know where the love of God goes
when the fish turn the minutes to hours?

As we reached the tailout, Lucky Porter and his two
clients appeared around the bend upriver, and began massaging the same run. When we hopped out of the boat to walk it
through a shallow riffle in the tailout, we heard a WOOT! from
Porter's boat. Joe Golcz, from Duluth, was in the bow and his rod
was doubled over. Porter was grabbing for the net and the back-
seat angler was stowing his rod and trying to stay out of the way.

When the fish was in the net, Porter double-timed it on
the oars and pulled in beside us. I was ready with my camera to
photograph Joe Golcz with his first-ever musky on his first-ever
day of musky fishing. She was a 46-incher with a massive girth
and the face of an alligator. Porter was ecstatic, Brad was waxing
poetic, and Joe still wasn't quite aware of what he'd accomplished.

After the release they gathered around my LCD screen
and we scrolled through the shots. Joe gave me his email address
and thanked me for being there.

On my flight home the next day I uploaded the shots
into my laptop and replayed the events surrounding a great fish.
I wondered if the musky had seen our flies. Surely she had, and
maybe our relentless casting is what got her lathered up? And
even though Brad bantered that Joe had reached the pinnacle of
musky fishing on his first attempt, maybe that fish was intended
for him all along?

Maybe Joe was the talent and Bob and I were nothing but
a couple of fluffers?

The End of Days

It's been four years, now, since the stock market lost half of its value in a gut wrenching three-month skid. We've started a slow climb from the worst depression since The Depression, but the overall mood in our country remains unsettled.

Unemployment is still up and housing starts are down. Manufacturing is tepid and oil prices are through the roof. Natural gas prices are at historic lows but Apple's stock price just tipped $600 share. And enhancing all of this ambiguity, it's an election year, so we're being force-fed an incessant crap casserole of political posturing and lies.

Over the past few years we've seen an austere collapse in the confidence of our government. A lot of people are broke and pissed off. Others have a little cash on hand but they're still pissed off. While those groups make up the biggest share of the

183

U.S. populace, there's another faction whose roster is rapidly expanding; the paranoid and pissed off—or as some like to call them, "Preppers."

They're the ones that are convinced that the apocalypse is imminent. Like tomorrow, or the next day, but certainly no later than next Friday, December 21, 2012. None of them can pinpoint its actual form but most believe that our government will have a hand in either causing it, or not preventing it.

I recently watched an episode of *Doomsday Bunkers* on Discovery. It's a new reality series based on the lives of various Preppers and those who have wisely positioned themselves to stoke their fears and cash in on their hand-wringing.

This particular episode featured a retired military man turned conspiracy theorist, who now travels the country teaching survival seminars to his brethren Preppers. He had a shaved head and wore skin-tight combat wear stretched over his chiseled frame. He had put down a deposit for the "ultimate survival bunker" and that transaction introduced us to the enterprising contractor who was charging a half-million dollars to build it for him.

The project would total 1,800 square feet comprised of three different structures for living, sleeping, and storage of food, guns, and ammo. There would be plumbed toilets, showers, and vanities supplied by a deep well beneath the structure. A massive generator and fuel tank would supply air conditioning, heat, and power. Video surveillance would tell the Preppers, at a glance, who was lurking outside and whether they had enough "ordinance" to penetrate the bunker's custom blast door. If they did, a turret gun controlled by a laptop and a joystick would take them out before they got their fuse lit.

Watching the broadcast, I felt a stirring range of emotions over its hour-long course:

First: *Are you fucking kidding me...an 1,800 square foot bunker?*

Followed by: *Whoa...do I need to build one of those...?*

And finally: *Wait a minute...these people are nutty as squirrels...*

By the end of the show I was basking in a warm and happy place without a shred of fear for what might happen if Congress gets any dumber, or if NASA fails to divert that giant space rock hurtling toward my house.

So what if the big one *does* hit? A bomb, a meteor, a pandemic, the black helicopter invasion, or a societal collapse caused by an inept government? If it's bad enough to whisk the family underground and live off powdered punch and canned weenies for 6-8 months, then what will it be like when it's finally safe to come up for a breath?

We've all seen the movies: *The Stand, Mad Max, The Day After Tomorrow, The Road*. While opinions may vary on what may eventually spawn the apocalypse, everyone seems to agree on the likely aftermath: the survivors will be doomed to wander a barren wasteland where gangs of thugs, and Tina Turner, scheme and kill for fuel, food, and human collateral.

So, let's say I decide to build a bunker for my wife and kids and we survive the apocalypse. When we emerge from below will there be anything left that resembles the life we previously knew?

Will vast hordes of tarpon still swim past Key West each spring? Will redfish still gang up in big waggling bunches on calm summer mornings in Port Aransas? Will there still be salmon streams in Alaska, BC steelhead, Bahamian bonefish, and reasonable means to reach those places? Will I be able to chuck a rod in my truck and poach a bass from a golf course pond within five minutes of my house?

Okay, forget fishing.

What about college football, and crisp fall weather, and weddings, and grandbabies, and Christmas, and Mexican food, and yellow labs?

I saw none of that in *Beyond Thunderdome*. So all we'll have left are these well-prepared wingnuts emerging from their bunkers and riddling each other with their supplies of ammo in hopes of wresting away the remaining stocks of Spam and toilet paper from other Preppers?

Thanks. I'll pass.

I'll buy a family pack of tickets for whatever tragedy befalls us if I can avoid the aftermath. Who wants to live with a bunch of hollering red-asses wearing tinfoil hats who will inherently distrust the next civilization before it ever rebuilds? What's the point of surviving if everything worth living for is gone?

Note: December 21, 2012 came and went without a ripple. Turns out that the Mayans didn't observe leap year so their calendar was never accurate anyway.

Confessions of a Fish Counter

The affliction started as a benign quest for knowledge.

No, really, it did.

———

In the fall of 1990, I caught my first redfish near Port Mansfield, Texas. There was a small knot of gulls hovering over a pod of tailers. Shrimp were jumping and tails were flopping and gulls were squawking, and when my line came tight I thought: *this is really fun and I need to do this more often.*

For the next few years I booked guides up and down the Texas Coast and caught more redfish. Though pricey, that program was working pretty well until my friend Will Myers said, "Hey, I've been fishing a few flats near Port Aransas by kayak. They're covered with redfish, come check it out." The word "kayak" immediately spawned images of seal skins and harpoons. I had no clue what Will was proposing but I was game to give it a try.

A few weeks later, in June of 1994, I met Will before daylight on the causeway near Port Aransas. Strapped to the roof of his Suburban were two long, skinny 14-foot plastic boats. They were a fairly new breed of roto-molded craft called "sit-on-tops." No spray skirts required. We slid them off his truck, strung up our rods, and paddled across the Shrimp Boat Channel to a system of shallow flats behind the Lydia Ann Lighthouse. About 20 yards into the first lake, Will slowed to a stop, motioned me forward, and pointed with his paddle.

"There."

"What?"

"Redfish."

"Where?"

"*There.*"

"Oh...dang."

Thirty feet off his bow was a pile of waggling redfish in a foot of water. Twenty feet beyond that was another group. As I looked out across the flat I could see more pods tailing up. It was almost as if someone had flipped a switch marked "DIG."

The lake we were fishing had a soft mud bottom laced with oyster reefs. It was too mucky for wading, so the kayaks provided a simple and stealthy means of approach.

For the next six hours Will and I paddled from one tailing pod to the next. When I got back to Austin I stopped at the local paddling shop and bought a sit-on-top kayak and a paddle and a roof rack for my truck. A week later I went back to the same flat and again found it crawling with redfish.

Since that day, I've spent an inordinate amount of time watching the weather, reading tide charts, juggling calendars, and driving back and forth between Austin and the coast. I like redfish in skinny water. And I especially like them when viewed from about three feet above the surface, which is where my eyes are when I'm sitting in my kayak. To me, their tailing, slurping, crawling, dashing, and waking is not nearly as exciting when viewed from the bow of a poling skiff.

The learning curve was steep in those early years, but I quickly found that water movement is everything to a redfish. No tide, no show. Redfish are lazy and they like current because current nudges the shrimp and the crabs and the baitfish into view.

In 1998 I took the deal a step further and bought a boat that I could use to ferry my kayak to new waters. That program opened up a lot of new territory beyond my comfy and familiar home flats.

I don't recall exactly when the idea came to me, but one day I grabbed a notebook and divided a page into columns. I labeled the columns: Date, Location, Starting Tide, Ending Tide, Temperature, Wind, and Fish.

My entirely innocuous plan was to begin jotting down some stats on each day of redfishing. I wanted to see if over time I could better predict fish movements based on tidal flow and the weather. No big deal, right? Lots of people keep fishing logs.

My hope was to eventually compile enough data so that

that my decision making on which flat to fish and what time to be there would become an ingrained reflex and not a blind swing in the dark.

You see where this going, don't you?

For the first few years of this program I filled up pages and columns of fishing data. And indeed, over time, I began to see certain patterns emerge. After 4-5 years my decision on where to fish became automatic. While drinking coffee each morning, I'd check the online tide tables to see which direction the water was moving. At the dock, before stepping into my boat, I'd check the actual water level on the pilings to make sure all was in sync. From there I'd head toward a flat or system of lakes where I knew I could catch an incoming tide with gluttonous redfish pushing in on the new water.

It was a great system, but it came with a price.

Over time, the column marked "Fish" became more important than the tide and weather data. Had I simply jotted down the day's catch and moved on, I'd have never contracted the disease. Looking back, I can point the finger of infection toward my computer. Transferring the data into Microsoft Excel was a good idea. Using the Sum and Average functions was a terrible mistake.

With those virulent computations in place I could quickly devise a daily average of redfish caught. I could divide the data into years and months and compare my catch rates from one season to the next. At first those numbers didn't mean much, but over time they completely consumed me. After each day of fishing I'd race home and log in my catch. I'd then check the daily average column and fix that number in my brain. The next time I went out, I had to meet or beat that number.

Sad, I know.

But it got worse. I started cherry picking my days and not fishing when the weather wasn't perfect. I stopped exploring new water and kept hammering the same flats that had produced well in previous years. I quit watching the birds and enjoying the sunrises and shooting photos of tailing schools.

I was a fish counter.

Oddly, though, at the height of my redfish tallying addiction, I wasn't keeping records on other species. There were no spreadsheets for tarpon, bonefish, or steelhead.

Just redfish.

Maybe it was because those species required plane tickets and guides and lodges? All I needed for redfish was a weather window and a paddle.

Whatever the impetus, the number had completely replaced everything that I loved about redfish. Most unsettling were those epic summers when the weather held and the fish tailed for days on end. The daily average would creep to new heights and I'd have to beat it. On days when the fish were really turned on, I'd hook one and immediately start looking for another tailer or cruiser before I landed the one I was fighting.

I was a tournament of one. A stoked-up number cruncher on a mission to snatch the trophy away from myself. I didn't have sponsors or logos; I was shrink-wrapped in data.

The years rolled by and the number grew. I've never written any articles about redfish, and I've only shared the number with a few people who have asked. But I kept on counting.

And fishing.

And counting.

But then one day I stopped.

Like Forrest Gump at the end of that really long jog, I just stopped.

———

It was a blazing hot day in July 2011 and the flats around Port Aransas were heating up to intolerable levels. The fish were up shallow and active right at daybreak but then they'd scoot into the creeks for a cooldown. I had caught a few fish early but by mid-morning they had scattered. I knew that the odds of catching more fish were slim but I kept on paddling and looking.

The number.

At noon it was pushing 100 degrees, there was no wind, and my boat was a speck on the horizon. I reached for my water bottle…and it was empty. I hadn't screwed the lid down tight after the last sip.

Damn.

The number.

I started paddling back toward my boat. After twenty minutes of stroking and sweating and gasping, I looked up and it didn't appear any closer. I pictured myself crawling in tattered clothes through the Sahara toward a shimmering mirage. I was miserable and I was pissed and I was embarrassed. I thought back to what my urologist said about staying hydrated. A phantom pain began building in my lower back.

When I finally reached the boat, I chugged two bottles of water, stowed my kayak, and motored back to Port Aransas. I had planned to fish one more day, but I didn't. I pulled the boat out of the water, hosed it down and drove back to Austin.

When I got home, I didn't tally my catch. For the first time in many years, I didn't care how many redfish I'd caught.

The heat wave continued through September and the flats never cooled down. And then the hunting seasons started and redfish were shelved for the year. Looking back, that hiatus was the treatment that I needed. A stark elixir of abstinence.

In April of 2012 we spent Easter weekend in Port Aransas. My son Blake was home from college and he was itching to fish. We launched on a bright calm morning and paddled a flat that I hadn't fished in years. There were scattered singles and a couple of tailing groups and I had a great time shooting photos of Blake.

By 11:30 the tide had gone slack and Blake said, "Dad, you haven't even picked up your rod."

"I know, let's swing past that grassy point on the way back to the boat. I've seen fish there, before."

Just past the point I found a single redfish working a clump of oysters. When my fly landed he moseyed over and gave it a sniff and then he turned and dashed away in a billowy mud plume.

I looked at Blake and he cringed and said, "Bummer."

But I didn't care because I wasn't going to write it down anyway.

Bonefish on a Budget

The flat totaled about 2,000 acres and was bound by a barrier island to the east, a dense mangrove swamp to the north and west, and an inlet creek to the south. Twice each day the creek would fill and drain the flat. With an average depth of about a foot, that's a lot of water movement between full high and dead low.

The tide was already in full retreat when I waded onto the flat at 6:00 a.m. It was late June, the sun was barely cracking the horizon, and I was already sweating through my shirt.

About 50 yards out from the beach, a single bonefish was noodling the bottom and spreading ripples across the mirrored surface. He'd kick and lunge and then his tail would knife up as he sucked some hapless critter from the sand. Between feeding events he would completely disappear in water barely deep enough to cover my ankles. He was working toward the creek and we both knew that time was not on our side. The mangrove roots were fully exposed and sand humps were beginning to emerge on the far side of the flat.

I stripped out line and began my approach and his attitude immediately changed. He didn't spook; he just began moving quietly away, pushing a bow wake and decreasing the odds of my getting off a cast. I was barefoot on a firm sandy bottom, but to him I probably sounded like someone clanking through a gymnasium with saucepans for shoes. I tried a cut-off angle that might allow us to meet before he reached the creek, but he was casually swimming at about twice the speed I was stalking.

Looking north I spotted two more fish working my way. They were still tailing and feeding, but with more urgency than they would on a flooding tide. The sun was up now and it was god-awfully hot and still and quiet. I crabbed a few yards to my left and stripped out enough line for a long shot. And then I stood like a heron and waited. I was between them and the creek and they'd have to pass within range. As I stood hoping for a shot, I looked down at my feet and watched the retreating tide. Tiny baitfish were scurrying past and a hermit crab was working towards its hole.

At seventy feet I lifted my rod to start my cast and the closer fish took off like a scalded ape. His pal must've been looking down because he didn't spook. I crouched low and started a sidearm windup, trying to keep the shadow of my fly line away from the fish. At fifty feet I dropped the fly in his path and waited. At forty feet I began my strip. At thirty-eight feet a horse fly jabbed its proboscis into my calf and the bonefish tailed on my fly at the exact moment that I reached down to slap that fucker dead.

I missed them both.

My backpack and my bug spray were about seventy yards to my right. Way uptide I could see a couple more tailers moving my way.

I reached the bank just as a hotel employee drove up to where I was parked. "How's it goin' Mista Brown?"

"Great, needing some bug spray."

"Yessah, them docta flies are baaaaad this time-a-yea."

"Yes they are, and we could use a little breeze, too."

"Yessah, looks like a glass table out theya. Any bonefish dis mawnin?"

"A few, but the tide's just about gone."

"Yessah, looks kinda shally."

I doused up with Deet and shoved the bottle in my pocket. "Well, I'm gonna give it another shot, there's still a few fish working toward the creek."

"Okay sah, good luck to ya!"

He watched as I turned and took a line that might get me in range of the last few stragglers.

"Oh, Mista Brown…?"

I turned and looked his way.

"The spa confirmed your wife's nail appointment for 1:00 today."

"Great, thank you. I'll tell her."

"No problem, sah. Can I get you somethin cool to drank?"

"That would be great, maybe a couple of waters?"

"No problem, sah. I'll fetch em and leave em hea'ya in ya golf cart."

And then he turned and whirred away in his. And I paused and tried to remember if bottled waters were $8 each on my bar chit, or only $6.50.

Access

The takeout downriver from Smithville was a dirt ramp behind a locked gate. We had permission, but I'm not sure how. Up the hill was a collection of single-wides, derelict RV's, rusted farm implements, and a Glastron ski boat on blocks.

When there came a god-awful squealing we thought the cable on the trailer winch was binding. We stopped cranking and listened and the sound was coming from up the hill. Just then a man came down the ramp with wild hair and bib overalls and not many of his uppers.

"How'd y'all do?"

"Good!"

"Bass or catfish?"

"All bass."

"White'uns or them regulars?"

"Just regulars."

"Crawdads?"

"No, flies."

He tugged at his asscrack and pondered flies and then he went on about he and his boy and a mess of "yallercats" they'd caught three nights back. He said they started off in the evening fishing for bass because, "They was going off like a jackass in a tin barn."

When the squealing started again we turned and looked up the hill, and then back at him.

"What's all that racket?"

"Dinner."

"*Dinner?*"

"Yeah. We got up on a hog."

Ebb Tide

Youth sports, when I was growing up, were arranged and administered by our local YMCA. I played football and basketball there in 6th grade.

In the third quarter of a basketball game, one Saturday morning, I was overcome with an urgent need to urinate and knew that I couldn't hold it until the final buzzer. I alerted my coach to the problem during a timeout and he waved me toward the restroom. In my haste to find a stall I somehow ended up in the men's locker room, and the freak show that I stumbled into there is still permanently affixed in my mind.

Standing about were several old men in various stages of undress. Skinny hairless legs, huge stomachs, flabby man tits, giant boxer shorts hiked up beneath armpits, and one scrotum so impossibly long that it looked fake. Mumbling something like,

"Oh sorry..." I spun out the door, ran back to the gym, and found my still-warm spot on the bench. I didn't need to pee anymore, nor did I for the remainder of that week.

Since that day I've had a nagging fear of geezerhood.

Will I look like those locker room refugees when I get old?

Do ALL old men look like that?

Thinking back, I have no idea exactly what age they were but I'm proud that at 50 I'm still in fair shape. My back and knees can't take as much wave-pounding or bow-standing as they once could, but I'm still wearing my pants at waist-level and I've never sat on my sack.

One suggestion, though: when you hit 45 and you begin stocking your boat, vehicle, and house with cheap reading glasses, go ahead and place a pair on the counter beneath your bathroom mirror. If you can't thread 2X through a #4 hook eye without magnification, then you won't be able to see those rowdy nose hairs, either. Especially the gray ones.

An interesting component of the aging process is the change in perception of what one considers necessary gear, versus superfluous clutter. I was once an unappeasable gear hound but those days are peeling away. I haven't completely transformed into a creaky old minimalist, but I do spend much less time flipping through gear catalogs, and a lot of them get tossed in the can without a sniff.

When I travel, I'm sometimes paired to fish with and photograph elderly gentlemen who could buy all of my camera gear with the loose bills in their dryer. Over time I've noticed an inclination of nostalgia that tends to pervade their packing for a trip. They'll typically ante up for new rods and reels when booking a pricey destination, but there's always something in their duffle from the Truman years with which they're having difficulty parting.

On a cold day in British Columbia a few years back, I fished with a delightful old codger wearing a $400 jacket who was shivering and miserable by 9 a.m. When asked if he wanted a fleece layer he gladly accepted and unzipped his jacket to reveal one of those old waffle-stamped cotton long john shirts that were long ago popular, yet never warm. He did catch a steelhead that day, but he didn't get a photo because the rain had soaked through his (circa 1963) L.L. Bean canvas shoulder bag and ruined his camera.

I suppose it's easy for me to critique his stuff from my position on the timeline, but two things are certain when it comes to my personal gear selection, nostalgia be damned.

First, I'm not well-programmed for cold weather so I will *always* be dressed to handle it. And second, because I'm a tight-wad who hates re-buying gear, mine will *always* be protected from any weather or human calamity I may face.

I've probably got enough rods (single-handed), reels, and gadgets to last me until the end of my days, but vendors take note: if on my death bed you can show me a pair of warm socks, a dry jacket, or a cool new gear bag that I don't have, I'll probably buy it.

Beyond the physical changes that come with aging, I've

recently noticed various points of stark enlightenment where I'm standing in a river, or on the bow of a skiff, and I suddenly realize that I will likely never get any better at that particular game.

At a point, things become ingrained; good habits and bad. Granted, redfish and bass are both abundant and convenient for me and it's likely that I'll continue to improve in those venues. When you reach midlife, though, and you only fish for bonefish a couple of days per year, then your upside on getting much better at bonefishing is somewhat limited.

I am not a great fly-caster. Never have been. I've usually managed to catch fish, but I don't recall many people stopping to watch.

There were no casting videos back in the seventies, and no fly shops within a half-day drive of my home. I once looked up "fly fishing" in the encyclopedia, but there wasn't much information beyond an enlightening brief on the origin of the verb "angle."

I learned to fly-cast by erroneous perception. If my fly landed quietly within a few yards of where I was aiming, that was a good cast, and the mechanics, by golly, just didn't matter.

During college I took a couple of lessons from the old Austin Angler fly shop. While those sessions did iron out a few of the more awful features of my cast, the damage was already done and many of my present-day quirks and jiggles were already acutely impressed.

My casting did improve when I started fishing saltwater, but even today I can sometimes feel a boatmate's bewildered glare drilling into the back of my head after I've made an unexplainably horrible cast.

Jeez, and this guy's been fishing for how long?

And it's not just casting. Remember that old hammer-sweep tarpon hookset that I referred to earlier? Muscle memory can be a cruel mistress.

As I continued fishing for tarpon over the years and the fish got smarter and the flies got smaller, that violent, pounding hookset that was once so popular began to fall out of favor. Nowadays the protocol is simple; when a tarpon eats a 1/0 needle sharp hook, just keep stripping. When the line comes tight, feed it out with tension and get him on the reel.

On a spring day in Key West, recently, my son Blake fell into a remarkably smooth groove of casting to and hooking tarpon. He caught every fish that ate his fly, that day, and he made it look easy.

On that same day I completely whiffed. It started when a big one rose from the glare directly beneath the boat and ate my fly on a short string. It scared the hell out of me, and my girly-man trout set would have racked up millions of clicks had someone been filming.

At that point I was done. Psyched out. It didn't matter how many tarpon I'd caught that week, or in the twenty years prior. On that day I was finished. Blake would catch a tarpon; then I'd miss one. Again, and again. On my last shot of the day I had a classic head-on follow. The tarpon rose, gulped the fly… and I hammer-swept it right out of its mouth.

Totally deflated, I turned and looked at Chris McCreedy, our guide, who tactfully offered, "A little too much rod, there, buddy."

Blake was sitting motionless on the cooler, and when our eyes met he responded with a sympathetic shrug and said, "Dad...just keep stripping."

Thanks, pal.

I intend to.

Starting tomorrow.

A Mid-Lifer's List

- I hope that humankind will grow in their understanding of the critical balance between consumption and protection of our natural resources.

- I hope that fishing tournaments will one day give away prizes so trivial that no one will act like a jackass to win them.

- I hope the IGFA will at some point close the record books on the progressively ludicrous pursuit of torturing bigger fish on lighter line.

- I hope that kids will someday tire of glowing screens and rediscover the outdoors.

- I hope that the entire Far Eastern populace will very soon develop an insatiable appetite for chicken.

- I hope that smart and honorable people will run for public office so we can vote out those who aren't.

- I hope that everyone on this planet will soon realize that fresh water is not something that we can manufacture to meet demand.

- I hope the networks will at some point revert back to reporting the news instead of creating it.

- I hope to catch a lot more fish, and one big snook.

- I hope to have grandkids someday, and I look forward to giving them each a fly rod.

Thanks

To Kathy, Blake, and Emily for your unwavering support of a career that didn't involve neckties and shiny shoes.

To the anglers who trusted my research and booked the destinations that I represented during the travel agency years.

To the guides, worldwide, of whom there are too many to name. I've learned something from each of you and I will always be an ardent supporter of your profession.

To the photo buyers and art directors who have licensed my photography and encouraged me to keep shooting.

To the lodges and outfitters who have made room for me, often during their busiest months, and allowed me to document and promote their operations.

To the publishers and editors who took chances on a Texan with a hazy understanding of proper semicolon use.